X XII/C

THE COL amous .

TENN

TE DERS

13 A

• *World Famous* •

GASLIGHT MURDERS

COLIN WILSON

with
Damon and Rowan Wilson

MAGPIE
London

Magpie Books Ltd
11 Shepherd House
Shepherd Street
London W1Y 7LD

First published in the UK
by Magpie Books Ltd in 1992

Copyright Robinson Publishing © 1992

ISBN 1 85487 153 6
ISBN 1 85813 089 1
10 9 8 7 6 5 4 3 2 1

Printed in Finland by
Werner Söderström Oy

364.152 3 W

070003 9

Contents

chapter one

THE AGE OF GASLIGHT

"*The Age of Gaslight*" – *the words evoke nostalgic images of Victorian music halls and Dickensian hotelries peopled by characters like Sam Weller and the Artful Dodger. In fact, coal gas had been invented at the end of the previous century. It is a fascinating story, and worth telling before we embark on our venture into Victorian murder.*

When Sir Archibald Cochrane became Earl of Dundonald in 1778, he had no money to go with the title – it had been dissipated by spendthrift ancestors. But at least he had a coal mine near his property at Culross Abbey, not far from Edinburgh. He began making tar for coating ships' bottoms, cooking coal in huge kilns. Unfortunately, the Admiralty decided to start protecting their ships with copper bottoms, and the Earl went bankrupt and died penniless. But while he was still experimenting with the tar-making process, he one day allowed a kiln to overheat. It exploded, and he noticed that the resulting gas burned brightly. If he had grasped the significance of what was happening, he might have ended a rich man instead of dying in a Paris slum. Unfortunately, the Earl lacked imagination.

But at least he passed on his interesting observation to a Scottish engineer called James Watt, who had invented a new and improved type of steam engine. Watt in turn mentioned it to his young assistant William Murdock, who sold steam engines in Cornwall. Murdock tried the simple experiment of heating coal in an iron container, and lighting the gas which came out of a pipe leading from the container. Watt liked the idea so much that two years later, in 1801, he installed the first two gas burners in his factory in Soho. The resulting smell became known as "the Soho stink".

FIFTY POUNDS
REWARD.

Horrid Murder!!

WHEREAS,

The Dwelling House of Mr. TIMOTHY MARR, 29, Ratcliff Highway, Man's Mercer, was entered this morning between the hours of Twelve and Two o'Clock, by some persons unknown, when the said Mr. MARR, Mrs. CELIA MARR, his wife, TIMOTHY their INFANT CHILD in the cradle, and JAMES BIGGS, a servant lad, were all of them most inhumanly and barbarously Murdered!!

A Ship Carpenter's Pem Maul, broken at the point, and a Bricklayer's long Iron Ripping Chissel about Twenty Inches in length, have been found upon the Premises, with the former of which it is supposed the Murder was committed. Any person having lost such articles, or any Dealer in Old Iron, who has lately Sold or missed such, are earnestly requested to give immediate Information.

The Churchwardens, Overseers, and Trustees, of the Parish of St. George Middlesex, do hereby offer a Reward of FIFTY POUNDS, for the Discovery and Apprehension of the Person or Persons who committed such Murder, to be paid on Conviction.

By Order of the Churchwardens, Overseers, and Trustees,

JOHN CLEMENT,
VESTRY CLERK.

Ratcliff-highway,
SUNDAY. 8th, DECEMBER, 1811.

SKIRVEN, Printer, Ratcliff Highway, London.

So the Age of Gaslight began long before Queen Victoria came to the throne in 1837. By 1805, many Manchester cotton mills were lit by gaslight. And by 1820, most major British towns were illuminated by its yellow, flickering flames, (Gas mantles were not invented until the beginning of the twentieth century, so gaslight looked rather like an outsize candle flame.)

At least gaslight made the street safer at night; throughout most of the eighteenth century, late travellers were likely to be attacked by footpads. The most shocking crimes of the early nineteenth century were committed behind closed doors, or in remote areas of the countryside where there was no gas.

The Ratcliffe Highway Murders

In 1811, there was a case that made a sensation through the length and breadth of the country, and caused householders everywhere to bolt and bar their shutters. It took place in a house in the Ratcliffe Highway, in the East End of London. On the night of Saturday, 7 December 1811, someone broke into the house of a hosier named Timothy Marr, and murdered Marr, his wife, their baby and an apprentice boy of thirteen. A servant girl who had been sent out to buy oysters discovered the bodies. The incredible violence of the murders shocked everyone; the family had been slaughtered with blows of a mallet that had shattered their skulls, then their throats had been cut. The killer was obviously a homicidal maniac, but the motive had probably been robbery – which had been interrupted by the girl's return. In an upstairs room, a constable of the river police found the murder weapon – a "maul", a kind of iron mallet with a point on one end of the head; they were used by ships' carpenters. The head had the initials "I.P." punched into it. Two sets of footprints were found leading away from the house.

Twelve days later, there was a second mass murder at a public house called the King's Arms, in Gravel Lane, close to the Ratcliffe Highway. The pub was run by a Mr Williamson and his wife, with help from their fourteen-year-old granddaughter, Kitty Stilwell, and a servant, Bridget Harrington. There was

VIEW OF THE BODY OF JOHN WILLIAMS
the supposed Murderer of the families of Marr and Williamson, and Self-destroyer, approaching the hole dug to receive it, in the Cross Road, at Cannon Street — Turnpike.

also a lodger, twenty-six-year-old John Turner. After the bar had closed at 11 p.m., Williamson served a drink to an old friend, the parish constable, and told him that a man in a brown jacket had been listening at the door, and that if the constable saw him, he should arrest him.

A quarter of an hour later, the lodger had gone to his bed in the attic when he heard the front door slam very hard, then Bridget Harrington's voice shouting "We are all murdered." There were blows and more cries. Turner crept downstairs – naked – and peered into the living room. He saw a man bending over a body and rifling the pockets. Turner went back upstairs, made a rope out of sheets tied together, and lowered himself out of the window. As he landed with a crash on the pavement – the "rope" was too short – he shouted breathlessly "Murder, murder!" A crowd quickly formed, and the parish constable prised open the metal flap that led into the cellar. At the bottom of some steps lay the body of the landlord, his head beaten in by a crowbar that lay beside him. His throat had been cut and his right leg fractured. In the room above lay the bodies

Crossroads at Cable street and Cannon Street Row where Williams was buried with a stake through his heart.

of Mrs Williamson and Bridget Harrington. Both their skulls had been shattered, and both had had their throats cut to the bone. The murderer had escaped through a rear window.

Dozens of sailors and men in brown jackets were arrested on suspicion, among them a young sailor named John Williams, who lodged at the Pear Tree public house in nearby Wapping. He was a rather good-looking, slightly effeminate youth with a manner that sometimes caused him to be mistaken for a "gentleman". There was no evidence against him. But when handbills with pictures of the maul were circulated, John Williams's landlord, a Mr Vermilloe (who happened to be in Newgate prison for debt) said that he recognized it as belonging to a Swedish sailor named John Peterson. Peterson was now at sea, so had a watertight alibi, but had left his chest of tools behind, in the care of Vermilloe.

John Williams was now suspect number one. He had been seen walking towards the King's Arms on the evening of the murders, and had returned to his lodgings in the early hours of the morning with blood on his shirt – he claimed this was the result of a brawl. The stockings and shoes he had worn had been carefully washed, but bloodstains were still visible on the stockings. Williams's room mates said he had no money on the night of the murders, but had a great deal on the following day.

Williams cheated the executioner by hanging himself in prison on 28 December 1811. An inquest declared that he was the sole murderer of the Marrs and the Williamsons – a verdict that may be questioned in view of the two pairs of footprints that were found leaving the Marrs' house. He was given a suicide's burial at a cross roads in East London, with a stake through his heart – the old superstition being that suicides could become vampires.

The details of the Ratcliffe Highway murders are rather less interesting than the effect they produced on the public. It was the first time in English history – probably in European history – that a crime had created widespread panic. Why? Because it was generally accepted that they were committed by one man. In fact, it is rather more probable that they were committed by two, or even by a gang – one witness who lived near the Marrs said he heard several men running away. If that had been believed, there would almost certainly have been no panic –

gangs of thieves were still a familiar hazard in 1811. It was this notion of a lone monster, a man who stalked the streets on his own, lusting for blood, that terrified everybody. Jack the Ripper turned this nightmare into reality seventy-seven years later. But in 1811, the "alienated" criminal had still not made his appearance.

Thurtell and Hunt

Three more cases would produce this same widespread, feverish public interest during the next two decades. The first was the murder of a sportsman and gambler named William Weare by two more members of the sporting fraternity, John Thurtell and Joseph Hunt. Thurtell, a man of strong character and imposing physical presence, was familiar on the race courses and at barefist boxing matches. Weare had won from him a considerable sum of money at billiards, and Thurtell was convinced he had cheated. So Weare was invited for the weekend to a cottage belonging to a man called William Probert, near Elstree. The four set out from London in two horse-drawn gigs – two-wheeled carriages – and as they arrived, Thurtell shot Weare in the face; the bullet bounced off his cheekbone and Weare begged for his life. Thurtell threw him down, cut his throat with a penknife, then jammed the pistol against his head so hard that it went into the brain, filling the barrel with blood and tissue. The body was then dumped in a pond, and the three men went into the cottage and had supper with Probert's wife and sister-in-law. The next morning, Thurtell and Hunt went to look for the pistol and penknife, without success; but as they left, two labourers found the weapons on top of a hedge. They reported the find to the Bow Street Runners, who soon discovered Weare's body in another pond, into which it had been moved. Probert quickly turned king's evidence, and so escaped. Thurtell was hanged, while Hunt was transported for life.

This commonplace murder aroused such widespread interest

that it was quickly turned into a play that was performed before crowded houses. A popular ballad of the time – which was sold at the execution – had the well-known stanza:

> They cut his throat from ear to ear
> His head they battered in.
> His name was Mr William Weare
> He lived in Lyons Inn.

But why *did* it arouse such horrified fascination? It may have been partly because Thurtell was such a well-known character in the sporting world. But it was more probably the violence of the murder – the cut throat, the pistol filled with brains. Again, the crime touched a sense of nightmare: the ruthless criminal who ignores the laws of God and man. Yet the sensation it caused is also evidence that society was changing fast. In Defoe's time, the murder of Weare would have been merely one more case to add to the *Newgate Calendar*. But things were different in 1823. In his *History of Crime in England* (1873), Luke Owen Pike says:

> "England in the beginning of the year 1820, when George III died, was already the wealthiest and, in many respects, the most civilized country in Europe . . . Stage coaches now traversed all the main roads, which were at length beginning to deserve comparison with the great engineering works given to us by the Romans . . . Canals intersected the country . . . All these changes were, in the main, opposed to crime."

In fact, crime was rising steadily – Major Arthur Griffiths estimates in *Mysteries of Police and Crime* that there was a ratio of one criminal to every 822 members of the population in 1828. But most of these crimes were the result of misery and poverty, of half-starved factory workers and out-of-work farm labourers. What shocked people about the crimes of John Williams and John Thurtell was that they were not the outcome of desperation. They were deliberately committed for personal gain, for self-satisfaction; in other words, they were acts of ego-assertion, like the crimes of Caligula or Gilles de Rais. The age of individual conscience, inaugurated by Bunyan and Wesley, was changing into the age of individual crime.

This was, in fact, something of an illusion. Williams – and possibly a companion – had merely committed murder in the course of robbery: a hundred similar cases could be cited from the previous century. Thurtell's murder was a commonplace gangland execution; Weare was a scoundrel, and all four of them were gamblers and crooks. But the public *wanted* to believe that these were monsters; it stimulated some nerve of morbidity, in an age that was becoming increasingly prosperous and increasingly mechanized.

Murder in the Red Barn

This also explains the excitement generated by the "Red Barn murder" of 1827. William Corder, a farmer's son who became a schoolmaster, allowed himself to be bullied into marrying Maria Marten, a mole-catcher's daughter who was known in Polstead, Suffolk, as the local tart. She had lost her virginity to one gentleman ("an unfortunate slip" says the *Newgate Calendar*) and then bore a bastard child to another. She also became pregnant to William's brother Thomas, but the child died soon after birth. After Thomas abandoned her, Maria had an affair with a "gentleman" named Peter Matthews, who thereafter paid her an allowance of £20 a year.

William seems to have been an oversensitive mother's boy who was harshly treated by his father and made to work on the farm for a minimal wage. His response was to become something of a petty crook – on one occasion he borrowed money from a neighbour "for his father" and spent it; on another, he secretly sold some of his father's pigs. He was sent away to London in disgrace, but returned to the farm when his brother Thomas was accidentally drowned trying to cross a frozen pond. He soon became Maria's lover, and they spent their evenings making love in the Red Barn on the farm.

Maria's quarterly £5 note disappeared mysteriously, probably into Corder's pocket, indicating that he continued to look for the easy way out of his problems. Maria became pregnant again in 1827, and gave birth to a boy; but the child was sickly, and soon died. Maria's father evidently felt that it was time she became an honest woman, and pressed Corder so hard that he agreed to be married. At which point, he seems to have experienced regrets, and looked, as usual, for the easy way out. He told Maria that they must be married in secret, and persuaded her to meet him in the Red Barn, dressed in a suit of his own clothes. On 18 May Maria kept her appointment in the Red Barn, and was never seen again. Corder returned home and told Maria's family that he had placed her in lodgings in Ipswich for the time being. He told other stories to other enquirers. Then, tired of the gossip, Corder slipped away to London, where he advertised for a wife in a newspaper. The result was a meeting with a young woman called Mary Moore, whom he married. She had enough money to set up a girls' school in Ealing; Corder bought himself some spectacles and became headmaster.

Meanwhile, in Polstead, Maria's mother had been having lurid dreams in which she saw Corder shoot Maria in the Red Barn and bury her there. Her husband recalled that Corder had been seen with a pick and shovel on the day his daughter disappeared, and went and dug at a spot where the earth had been disturbed; he soon unearthed his daughter's body in a sack.

Corder was arrested and hanged – it was an open-and-shut case. His defence – that Maria had committed suicide during a quarrel – deceived no one. Before being hanged, in August 1828, he confessed to murdering Maria Marten.

A book and a play about the murder became instantly popular, and remained so into the twentieth century. Why? Men who killed their pregnant mistresses or wives were by no means uncommon. What thrilled the British public was the piquant mixture of sex and wickedness – the combination that still sells many Sunday newspapers. The *New Newgate Calendar* adopts an almost breathless tone: "The murder for which this most diabolical criminal merited and justly underwent condign punishment, rivalled in cold-blooded atrocity that of the unfortunate Mr Weare, and was as foul and dark a crime

William Corder, his victim Maria Marten and Maria's baby.

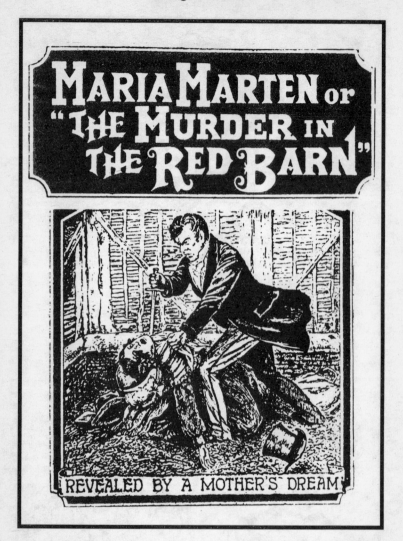

as ever stained the annals of public justice." Then it goes on to describe what a beautiful and "superior" young lady Maria was. In short, it has little or no relation to the actuality – a sluttish countrygirl of loose morals and a weak young man of criminal tendencies. But it was the story everybody wanted to believe, just as they wanted to believe that the "unfortunate Mr Weare" was a respectable businessman who had been lured to his death by two monsters.

A popular rhyme at the time of the Burke and Hare murders went:

"Burke's the murderer, Hare's the thief
And Knox the boy who buys the beef."

Burke and Hare

But at least cases like this made the British public aware of the need for a real national police force, instead of local parish constables. And the trial that, more than any other, brought this home to even the most anti-authoritarian liberals was that of the Edinburgh body-snatchers, Burke and Hare. These two Irish labourers met in 1826, and moved into a "beggars' hotel" in Tanner's Close, Edinburgh, together with their common-law wives. Somehow, Hare succeeded in taking over the house when its owner died. And when a tenant called Old Donald died owing his rent, Hare decided to recover the money by selling his corpse to the medical school. The dissection of bodies was forbidden by law; so when someone offered the medical schools a corpse – usually stolen from a newly-dug grave – no one asked any questions. Dr Knox, of 10 Surgeon's Square, paid Hare £7.10s for the corpse, which was more than twice what Old Donald owed. It struck Burke and Hare that this was an easy way of making a living – if only they could come by enough corpses. But graveyards were usually guarded to prevent the theft of bodies. The solution seemed to be to "make" corpses. So when a tenant called Joe the Mumper fell ill, Burke and Hare hastened his end by pressing a pillow over his face. The £10 they received for his body convinced them that they had stumbled upon a more profitable occupation than labouring.

In February 1828, a female vagrant named Abigail Simpson was lured to the house and made drunk. On this first occasion, Burke and Hare lost their nerve, and she was still alive the next morning. But they got her drunk again, and Hare suffocated her, while Burke held her legs. Again, the corpse was sold for

> **The early "bobbies" wore top hats lined with steel – not to protect their heads in case of attack, but so that they could stand on them if looking over a wall or through a window above head level.**

£10. And over the next eight months, they despatched eleven more victims by the same method. Some of the victims were never identified – like an Irish beggar woman and her dumb grandson; Burke strangled her and broke the boy's back over his knee. Dr Knox probably became suspicious when he was offered the body of an attractive little prostitute named Mary Paterson and one of his students recognized her as someone he had patronized. His suspicions must have become a certainty when Burke and Hare sold him the body of a well-known idiot called Daft Jamie, but he preferred to keep quiet.

The downfall of Burke and Hare came through carelessness; they left the corpse of a widow named Docherty in the house while they went out, and two of their lodgers located it. On their way to the police, they were met by Burke's common-law wife, who saw from their faces that something was wrong and fell on her knees to beg them to keep quiet. The tenants allowed themselves to be persuaded over several glasses of whisky in a pub, but finally went to the police anyway. A search of the house in Tanner's Close revealed blood-stained clothing. Hare quickly turned king's evidence and was not tried. Burke was sentenced to death, and hanged in January 1829. Hare left Edinburgh, and died, an old blind beggar, in London.

This was by far the most gruesome case in British criminal history; yet it was perhaps a little too horrifying for the British public, which preferred tales in which beautiful girls were seduced. So the case of Burke and Hare never achieved the same widespread popularity as the Red Barn murder, or the case of Ellie Hanley, the "Colleen Bawn" ("white girl"), a pretty Irish girl who had been married and then murdered by a young rake in 1819. But it undoubtedly helped to reconcile the British public to the first appearance of the British bobby (so called after the founder of the force, Sir Robert Peel) in September 1829. The new police were told to be firm but conciliatory, respectful, quiet and determined, and to maintain a perfectly even temper. They followed these instructions to the letter,

William Burke.

William Hare.

with the result that the public gradually lost its distrust of its new guardians.

Police Murders

But it took some time. During these early years, the major problem for the British bobby was simply that he wore uniform and looked "official". This tended to arouse automatic resentment in the slums of England's major cities. In June 1830, Police Constable Grantham saw two drunken Irishmen quarrelling over a woman in Somers Town, north London, and when he tried to separate them was knocked to the ground and kicked in the face with heavy boots. He died soon afterwards, the first British policeman to die in the execution of his duty; the murderers walked away and were never caught. Six weeks later, a policeman named John Long became convinced that three suspicious-looking characters in London's Gray's Inn Road were contemplating burglary, and accosted them. Two of them grabbed him by the arms and one stabbed him in the chest. There was a hue and cry, and another policeman who came on the scene caught a man who was running away. He proved to be a baker called John Smith, who had a wife and six children, and he protested that he had heard a cry of "Stop thief" and joined in the chase. His story was disbelieved and he was hanged a few days later. Under the circumstances, it seems likely he was innocent, and that the early police felt it was better to hang an innocent man than no one at all.

In 1833, the murder of another policeman revealed that the English attitude towards authority remained ambivalent. A mildly revolutionary group called the National Political Union called a meeting in Coldbath Fields, which was promptly banned by the police commissioner. The ban was ignored, and a crowd gathered around a speaker on a soap box. Eight hundred policemen and troops looked on suspiciously. A police spy slipped away from the crowd to report that sedition was being preached, and the man in charge of the police ordered his men to advance slowly, their truncheons at the ready. The crowd booed and pelted them with stones; the police got angry and began hitting out wildly, knocking down women and children as well as men. A man drew a knife as a policeman tried to capture an anarchist banner, and stabbed him in the chest. Police Constable Robert Culley staggered a few yards and fell dead.

A coroner's jury, considering the death, was obviously unsympathetic to the police, feeling they had no right to interfere with freedom of speech. When the coroner was told the jurors were unable to agree on a verdict, he replied that they would have to stay there without food and drink until they *did* agree. Whereupon the jury – which consisted of respectable

Burke and Hare at their trade.

tradesmen – produced a verdict of justifiable homicide against the unknown person who had stabbed Constable Culley. The spectators cheered, and the jury found themselves treated as heroes. The short-term result was to increase the hostility between police and public; but the long term-result was to allow Englishmen to stand on a soap box and say whatever they liked.

Crime in France: the Great Vidocq

In France, the whole situation would have been regarded as preposterous. They had had their official police force since the time of Louis XIV and the policeman took it for granted that he represented the king's authority and could say and do as he liked. One result of this attitude, of course, was the French Revolution. But the infamous Chambre Ardente affair, with its revelation of mass poisoning and child-sacrifice was evidence that the French needed a police force rather more urgently than the English. (This was, of course, before the introduction of gin caused the English crime wave.) The French chief of police was also the censor of the press, and could arrest newspaper publishers and anyone who printed a "libellous book". (Prohibited books were actually tried, condemned, and sent to the Bastille in a sack with a label – specifying the offence – tied to it.)

The French concentrated on the spy system to keep crime in check – a vast network of informers. M. de Sartines, the police minister under Louis XV, once had a bet with a friend that it would be impossible to slip into Paris without knowledge of the police. The friend – a judge – left Lyons secretly a month later, and found himself a room in a remote part of the city; within hours, he had received a letter by special messenger, inviting him to dinner with M. de Sartines. On another occasion, de Sartines was asked by the Vienna police to search for an Austrian robber in Paris; he was able to reply that the robber was still in Vienna, and give his exact address – at which the Vienna police found him.

The French underworld was also more organized than the

British could ever hope to be. When Louis XVI married Marie Antoinette in 1770, a gang stretched cords across the street under cover of darkness, and crowds attending the celebrations stumbled over them in large numbers. Two thousand five hundred people were trampled to death in the confusion, and the pickpockets moved around rifling the corpses. But the next day, de Sartines's men swooped on known criminals and made hundreds of arrests. They did it so swiftly that they recovered enormous quantities of stolen goods – watches, rings, bracelets, purses, jewellery – one robber had two thousand francs tied up in his handkerchief. It was an inauspicious beginning for a marriage that ended on the guillotine.

After the Revolution of 1789, the police force was disbanded – only to be formed again by Robespierre, who wanted to know what his enemies were doing. Napoleon appointed the sinister Joseph Fouché his police minister, and Fouché's spy network became even more efficient than that of de Sartines.

Under Fouché, the chief of police in Paris was a certain M. Henry. One day in 1809, he received a visit from a powerfully-built young man called Eugène-François Vidocq, who offered information about certain criminals in exchange for immunity. Vidocq was totally frank with Henry; his life had been adventurous, and a hot temper and a love of pretty women had brought him more than his share of trouble with the law. He had been a smuggler, and had escaped from prison, and even from the galleys. Now he wanted a quiet life. Henry could see Vidocq felt trapped; but he wanted him to feel still more trapped, until he would do anything that was asked of him. So M. Henry declined his offer and allowed him to go.

What Vidocq had not told Henry was that he was now involved with a gang of coiners. They denounced him to the police, who called when Vidocq was in bed; he was arrested, nearly naked, on the roof. When M. Henry saw the prisoner, he felt pleased with himself; now Vidocq was well and truly trapped. Henry was now able to state his own terms. And they were that Vidocq should become a police spy and betray his associates. It was hard, but Vidocq had no alternative than to accept. He was taken to the prison of La Force, with the task of spying on his fellow prisoners. It was dangerous work, but freedom depended on doing it well. He did so well, reporting undetected crimes to M. Henry, and the whereabouts of stolen goods, that M. Henry decided to give him his freedom – as a police spy. Vidocq was loaded with chains for transfer to another prison; on the way he was allowed to escape. It made him the hero of the criminal underworld of Paris. His first task was to track down a forger named Watrin, who had escaped and totally disappeared. Cautious enquiries revealed that Watrin had left some possessions in a certain room. Vidocq waited for him to reappear, captured him after a desperate struggle, and dragged him off to M. Henry. There was a large reward. Soon after, Watrin was guillotined. So was another forger named Bouhin – the man who had denounced Vidocq to the police two years earlier. He had been arrested on Vidocq's information.

During the next few years, Vidocq showed himself to be the most determined, efficient and enterprising police agent in Paris. His success aroused intense jealousy in the Police Prefecture, and his colleagues often denounced him as a man who was really in league with the criminals. M. Henry knew better; he knew Vidocq was too attached to his new-found security. He also knew that the rivalry between his men was the greatest threat to the efficiency of the Paris police. Every area in the city had its local station, and there was little co-operation between them. So when Vidocq suggested forming a small force of men who could move freely anywhere in the city, Henry immediately seized upon the idea. Vidocq was allowed four helpers, all chosen by himself – naturally, he chose criminals. There was fierce opposition from all the local police departments, who objected to strangers on their "patches", but Henry refused to be moved. Vidocq's little band was called the Security – Sûreté – and it became the foundation of the French national police force of today.

In 1833, Vidocq was forced to retire, because a new chief of police objected to a Sûreté made up entirely of criminals and ex-criminals. He immediately became a private detective – the first in the world – and wrote his *Memoirs*. He became a close friend of writers, including Balzac, who modelled his character Vautrin on Vidocq.

For the modern reader, the most astonishing thing about Vidocq's *Memoirs* is that the crimes were so singularly un-vicious. This is not to say that criminals were not perfectly capable of murder; only that there was a complete absence of the kind of anti-social resentment that distinguishes so many modern criminals. Burglary or robbery with violence was simply a profession, usually embraced by people who drank too much and liked to keep more than one mistress. Many robbers swore to "get" Vidocq when they came out; no one actually tried it, for their resentment evaporated quickly. During his early days as an informer, Vidocq met two hardened criminals he had known in jail, spent twenty-four hours drinking with them, and agreed to take part in a robbery which would include cutting the throats of two old men. He managed to get a note to M. Henry, and the police were waiting for them as they climbed over a garden wall. Someone fired; Vidocq dropped to the ground, pretending to be hit. And one of his fellow burglars had to be restrained from flinging himself in sorrow on Vidocq's "body". Vidocq often took the trouble to get to know men he had been instrumental in sending to the guillotine or life-imprisonment, performing small services – like taking messages to families – and formed genuinely warm and close relationships with them. He even instituted a custom of standing in the prison yard to watch the men being chained together before they were led off to the galleys. On the first occasion, they raged at him like wild beasts and dared him to come among them. Vidocq did precisely that – while prisoners looking out of barred windows urged the convicts to kill him. Yet no one touched him; they respected his bravery. Vidocq accepted various small commissions – final messages to wives and sweethearts – and parted from the convicts on the friendliest of terms. The socialists were obviously not entirely mistaken to argue that crime was largely a question of social conditions. The criminal with a "grudge against society" had not yet made his appearance.

Lacenaire

On 16 December 1834, a neighbour of the Widow Chardon, who lived at 271 rue St Martin, noticed a red stain that had seeped under the door, and when his knocks brought no reply, he went to summon the police. They discovered the corpse of a man lying in a pool of blood, his head split open by a hatchet, which lay next to the body. In the next room they found the body of an old woman, covered with stab wounds. She was the mother of the murdered man, who was a homosexual begging letter writer, nicknamed "Auntie". "It was on abject creatures known to share his tastes," says the disapproving Canler, "that suspicion first fell. Several of these filthy fellows were arrested and then released for want of proof." And, for the time being, the police investigation met an impasse.

Two weeks later, on New Year's Eve, Chief Inspector Canler was summoned to investigate an attempted murder. A young bank messenger named Genevey had been asked to call at 66 rue Montorgueil to collect money from a gentleman named Mahossier. On the fourth floor, the clerk found a room with "Mahossier" chalked on the door and knocked. As he entered the room, the door was closed behind him, and some sharp instrument was driven into his back. At the same time, a man tried to grasp him by the throat; he was clumsy, and his hand went into the clerk's mouth. Genevey was a robust young man; he struggled violently and shouted. His assailants became alarmed and ran away. Genevey staggered into the arms of neighbours who came to investigate.

At this time, the Sûreté – Paris's equivalent of Scotland Yard – was a modest organization, with a mere twenty-seven men: it had been founded a few decades earlier by a crook-turned-thief-catcher named Vidocq. Now its chief was a man named Pierre Allard, and he lost no time in appointing Canler to investigate both cases. He began by getting a good description of one of the assailants: a well-dressed man with a high forehead and a silky moustache; his manner, apparently, was polished and courteous. Significantly, he had been carrying a copy of Rousseau's *Social Contract*, the book that had virtually caused the French Revolution. The landlord at rue Montorgueil had not noticed the other man.

Now Canler proceeded to apply the needle-in-the-haystack method. It involved, quite simply, paying a visit to every cheap hotel and doss house in the Paris area, and asking to see the register that they were obliged to keep. Of course, it was obvious that "Mahossier" was not the man's real name, but Canler's knowledge of the criminal classes told him that they often used the same alias many times. And eventually, after trying every lodging-house in Montmartre, Île de la Cité, and the Temple area, he found what he wanted in rue du Faubourg du Temple: the name "Mahossier" in the hotel register. The proprietor shook his head; he had no memory of Mahossier. "How about this name underneath – Fizellier?" The proprietor, a man named Pageot, called his wife, and she was able to tell Canler that Fizellier was a big, red-haired man. Canler could sense that Pageot was not pleased by his wife's helpfulness; he didn't believe in helping the police more than necessary. So Canler thanked them and took his leave.

The description of Fizellier had rung a bell. A big, red-haired man had recently been arrested on a fraud charge, and he was at present in the central police station. Canler's expression was guileless as he entered his cell, notebook in hand, and pretended to search for a name:

"François, you tell me you're innocent of this fraud?"

"That's so."

"All right, then why did you call yourself Fizellier when you stayed at Mother Pageot's?"

"Because there was a warrant out for me, and I'd have been stupid to use my real name."

With quiet satisfaction, Canler went back to his office and made out a report stating that François was one of the two men in the bank messenger case. Then he returned to Mother Pageot's. This time he found her alone, and willing to tell what she knew. Mahossier, it seemed, had a high forehead and silky moustache, and he had stayed there before under the name of Bâton.

There *was* a crook called Bâton, a homosexual thief. "Fizellier" and "Mahossier" had shared a bed, so this might be the man. Canler ordered his arrest. But as soon as he saw him, he knew this was not Mahossier; Bâton was anything but distinguished or courteous. But again, Canler used his knowledge of criminal psychology. If Mahossier had borrowed Bâton's name, then he probably knew him. So, leaving Bâton in custody, Canler made a round of his haunts, and questioned his friends about a distinguished man with a silky moustache. A number of them agreed that this sounded like a person named Gaillard, with whom Bâton had been in prison. Back went Canler to Bâton, told him he was free to go, then asked him in a casual, friendly way about his friend Gaillard. Bâton's description left

no doubt that Gaillard and Mahossier were the same person.
But where was Gaillard? As soon as Canler began his enquiries,
he encountered a difficulty; there were several suspicious characters called Gaillard, and it might be any of them. So, with
infinite patience, Canler went back to searching the registers
of doss houses. It took him two days to find the signature
he wanted, in a hotel in the rue Marivaux-des-Lombards. The
proprietress remembered M. Gaillard, a tall man with a high
forehead. He had been visited occasionally by a lady. And he
had left behind a bundle of Republican songs in his room. She
still had them. And they made Canler aware of an interesting
aspect of his suspect's character – he was a poet, and not entirely
without talent. A letter in the form of a satirical poem made
some libellous aspersions about the previous prefect of police.
And the handwriting was unmistakably that of Mahossier.

Canler was now told that a prisoner named Avril wanted
to talk to him. Avril had heard on the grapevine that Canler
wanted to interview Gaillard. He offered to do a deal. If Canler
would like to release him, then have him discreetly followed,
he would wander around Gaillard's old resorts and see if he
could locate him. Canler agreed, and for the next week, Avril
was shadowed as he wandered from bar to bar. But when, at
the end of that time, there was still no sign of Gaillard, Canler
decided he was wasting police expenses, and had Avril put
back in jail.

Meanwhile, red-headed François had been convicted, and
was doing time in the Sainte-Pélagie prison. Canler decided
it was time to renew the pressure. But as he sat beside the
prisoner in the cabriolet taking them back to Canler's office,
François decided to speak of his own accord. He told Canler
that he could give him information about the murder of the
Chardons. He had spent an evening drinking with a man who
told him that he had murdered the Chardons, while one of his
acquaintances kept watch. The man's name? Gaillard . . .

And now, for the first time, Canler realized that his two cases
were connected. Mahossier had murdered the Chardons, and
attempted to murder and rob the bank messenger. In each crime
he had had a different accomplice. In the bank messenger case
it had been red-headed François. And in the murder case,
Canler had a hunch that the accomplice had been Avril.
Now he questioned Avril further, and obtained a new piece

of information. "Gaillard" had an aunt, old and quite rich, who lived in the rue Bar-du-Bec; he was even able to tell Canler the number. Canler's chief, Allard, was now so interested in the case that he went with him to visit the old lady. When they rang the bell of her apartment, a panel slid open, and a woman asked them what they wanted. "To speak to Madame Gaillard about her nephew. We are police officers."

In her apartment, Mme Gaillard explained apologetically that she did not trust her nephew, which was why she had had the grill put in the door – he was perfectly capable of murdering her. What, asked Allard, was her nephew's real name? "Pierre-François Lacenaire." It was the first time that Canler had heard the name of the criminal he was hunting for the past three weeks.

A general alert went out. There was no sign of Lacenaire in Paris. But a few days later, on 2 February 1835, the District Attorney in Beaune wrote a letter announcing the arrest of Lacenaire on a charge of passing a forged bill of exchange. He was brought back to Paris in chains. The man Canler and Allard confronted in his cell did not look like a master criminal – more like a gentleman down on his luck. When accused of the attempted robbery of the bank messenger, he admitted it without emotion; like many villains, he felt that it was simply a "job" that had turned out badly, like any unfortunate business venture. Asked the name of his accomplice, he replied: "Gentleman we villains have our code. We do not denounce our accomplices." Canler replied that his accomplices were not bound by a similar code; François had already betrayed him. Lacenaire merely smiled politely; he knew the police were capable of bluffing. All he would say was: "I shall make enquiries." He looked slightly more disturbed when Canler told him that Avril had done his best to betray him, but made the same response. Lacenaire was then transferred to La Force prison.

There his "enquiries" led to his being savagely beaten up by friends of François, so that he had to spend some weeks in the prison hospital. When he next saw Canler, he was ready to obtain his revenge. He made a full confession of both crimes, implicating Avril in the murder of the Chardons, and François in the attack on the bank messenger.

In prison, Lacenaire became a celebrity. The idea of a poetic murderer appealed to the Parisian public; he received many visitors, and discoursed to them on the injustice of the social system – to which he attributed his choice of a life of crime. In the period of the unpopular July Monarchy, with its repressive laws, this kind of thing appealed to Republican intellectuals. Lacenaire revelled in the limelight – it was what he had always craved. The poet Théophile Gautier called him "the Manfred of the gutter" (referring to Byron's noble rebel) and the nickname seemed appropriate. (Pictures of Lacenaire make him look rather like Poe.) In November 1835, Lacenaire, François, and Avril went on trial; Lacenaire and Avril were sentenced to death, François to life imprisonment. Lacenaire admitted frankly that his motive in giving evidence against his accomplices was revenge; he evidently took pleasure in making them aware that if they had observed the code of honour among thieves, none of them would have been in this predicament.

In prison, Lacenaire wrote his *Memoirs*, which were intended to be his justification. He is intent on proving that he is less a criminal than an "Outsider". "A victim of injustice since infancy . . . I had created a view of life very different from other men's. I know only one virtue, which is worth all the rest: it is Sensibility." In fact, the book is full of the emotional, upside-down logic of the typical criminal, a logic based upon self-pity. He loathed his father, and was upset because his parents preferred his elder brother; convinced at the age of sixteen that he would die on the guillotine (to which he liked to refer as his "mistress") he decided to "have the blood of society". But it soon becomes clear that his real trouble was not his philosophy of revolt, but his weakness; when things went well, he was a law-abiding citizen; as soon as they went wrong, he was thrown into a passion of indignation against fate, and tried to take the easy way out by looking around for something to steal. He lacked the ability to face adversity. It is worth commenting on this aspect of Lacenaire's psychology, for we shall encounter it many times in the course of this book.

The execution was carried out, unannounced, on a cold and foggy January morning. Lacenaire watched Avril's head fall into the basket without flinching; but when he himself knelt under the blade, there was an accident that would have broken another man's nerve; as the blade fell, it stuck half-way, and had to be hauled up again; Lacenaire was looking up at it as it dropped and severed his head.

• chapter two •

CRIMINAL TRIALS

*T*he *"Age of Gaslight" sounds almost modern – after all, it is the age before the coming of electricity. But you only have to read any account of trials in the early nineteenth century to realize that life was closer to the Middle Ages than to the twentieth century.*

The Bavarian judge Anselm Ritter von Feuerbach, who was active during the first three decades of the nineteenth century, also wrote a vast work consisting of the trials in which he had been concerned. A small part of it was translated into English in 1846 under the title Narratives of Remarkable Criminal Trials, *and it conveys more clearly than any work of history what it was like to live in Bavaria around the turn of the nineteenth century.*

The first case in this chapter is so typical that it is worth describing at length, even though the crime itself is brutal and horrific. Let Feuerbach himself set the scene, in order to give some idea of the flavour of his style.

The Case of John Paul Forster

"Christopher Bäumler, a worthy citizen of Nürnberg, lived in the Königsstrasse, a wide and much-frequented street, where he carried on the trade of a corn-chandler, which there includes the right of selling brandy. He had lately lost his wife, and lived quite alone with only one maid-servant, Anna Catherina Schütz. He had the reputation of being rich.

Bäumler was in the habit of opening his shop at five o'clock in the morning at latest. But on the 21st of September, 1820, to the surprise of his neighbours it remained closed till past six. Curiosity and alarm drew together a number of people before the house. They rang repeatedly, but no one came to the door. At last some neighbours, with the sanction of the police, entered the first-floor windows by a ladder. Here they found drawers, chests, and closets burst open, and presenting every appearance of a robbery having been committed. They hastened down stairs into the shop, where they discovered in a corner close to the street-door the bloody corpse of the maid; and in the parlour they found Bäumler lying dead beside the stove.

As soon as the police were informed of the murder, a commission was appointed to visit Bäumler's house. Immediately on entering the shop, to the right of the door in the corner, between two bins of meal and salt, the maid-servant Schütz lay on her back, with her head shattered, and her feet, from which both her shoes had fallen, turned towards the door. Her face and clothes, and the floor, were covered with blood; and the two bins, between which her head lay, as well as the wall, were sprinkled with it. As no other part of the shop showed any marks of blood, it was evident that she had been murdered in this corner. Not far from the body they picked up a small comb, and at a little distance from that a larger one, with several fragments of a second small one. In the very farthest corner of the parlour, between the stove and a small table, upon which stood a jug, they found the body of Bäumler stretched on his back, with his head, which was resting on a small over-turned stool, covered with wounds and blood. A pipe and several small coins lay under the body, where they had probably fallen when the murderer ransacked the pocket, which was turned inside out and stained with blood, for money or for keys. The floor, the stove, and the wall were covered with blood, the stool was saturated, and even the vaulted ceiling, which was nine or ten feet high, was sprinkled with it. These circumstances, especially the stool on which Bäumler's head still rested, and the pipe which lay under his body, showed that the murderer must have suddenly attacked him unawares and felled him to the earth, as he sat drinking his beer and smoking his pipe on that very spot.

On the table, in the parlour, stood a wine-glass with some red brandy at the bottom, and a closed clasp-knife stained with blood on the back and sides. Two newly-baked rolls were found near the entrance-door.

The baker Stierhof stated that Bäumler's maid had fetched these rolls from his shop the evening before, at about a quarter to ten. His wife, who was examined the next day on this point, recognised the rolls as those bought by the unfortunate maid-servant on the evening of the 20th of September.

On examining the body of the maid-servant, a handsome well-shaped girl of twenty-three, the head was found completely shattered; there were also several wounds upon the neck, breast, and hands, and the breast-bone and three of the ribs were fractured. Bäumler's skull was broken into eleven pieces; and although there were no external injuries upon the chest, the sternum and ribs were fractured, as in the maid-servant. There could not be the slightest doubt that the wounds were mortal. The surgeons gave it as their opinion that the wounds on the heads of both victims had been inflicted with a heavy instrument having a flat surface with sharp edges, probably the back of a hatchet. The ribs did not appear to have been broken with the hatchet, but rather by stamping on the bodies.

The evidence of the baker's wife had led to the conclusion that some man who had stayed until late in the evening at Bäumler's house must have been the murderer. Accordingly, all those who had been at Bäumler's house on that evening were examined, and concurred in saying that a stranger had entered the shop very early, had sat at the farther end of the table, alternately smoking and drinking red brandy out of a wine-glass; and that he had remained there alone at nine o'clock, when the others went away. All agreed in their description of his person; that he was about thirty, of dark complexion, and black hair and beard; that he wore a dark-coloured coat (most of the witnesses said a blue one, which afterwards proved to be a mistake), and that he had on a high beaver hat. With the exception of one witness who had conversed with the stranger about the hop trade and other like matters, and had found him a well-informed, agreeable man, they all stated that he had kept his hat pressed over his face, and his eyes constantly fixed on the ground, and that he had said little or nothing. He stated himself to be a hop-merchant, and said that he was waiting at Bäumler's for his companion, another hop-merchant, who had gone to the play. The witnesses recognised the glass produced in court, as exactly similar to that out of which the stranger had been drinking red clove-brandy."

The first thing that strikes the modern reader about all this is that Bäumler opened his shop at 5 a.m., and that the neighbours wondered what was the matter when he still wasn't open by 6. Elsewhere in the narrative, Feuerbach mentions that the brandy shop stayed open until 11 at night. An eighteen hour day. And it was obviously taken for granted by the rest of the people of Nuremberg, who probably worked roughly the same hours . . .

Feuerbach goes on to say:

"Meanwhile suspicion had fallen upon a certain Paul Forster, who had lately been discharged from the bridewell at Schwabach, and who had been observed for several days before the murder walking about in a suspicious manner before Bäumler's house. His father, a miserably poor day-labourer, lived with two daughters of infamous characters in a cottage belonging to a gardener named Thaler, in the suburb of St John. Forster did not live with his father; but on the morning after the murder he had left the suburb of St John quite early, and had gone to Diesbeck, where he lived with a woman called Margaret Preiss, who had been his mistress for many years. At her house he was arrested by the police on the 23rd of September, the third day after the murder. In her room were found, among other things, two bags of money, the one containing 209 florins 21 kreuzers, the other 152 florins 17 kreuzers. Besides these Preiss's illegitimate daughter, a girl of about fourteen, gave up a small purse containing some medals and a ducat which Forster had given to her when he returned to Diesbeck.

On the following day, when the gens d'armes were escorting Forster and his mistress through Fürth, the waiter of the inn recognised the prisoner as the man who had come to the inn at about eight or nine in the morning of the 21st of September, dressed in a dark grey cloth greatcoat, went away again in about an hour, and then returned dressed in a dark blue coat, and gave him a brown one which he carried under his arm to take care of, requesting him to keep it safe, and to be sure not to show it to any one; adding that in a week he would return and claim it. The waiter now informed the magistrate at Fürth of this circumstance, and produced the greatcoat, which was much stained and in some places soaked with blood.

The description given of the suspicious-looking stranger, who had sat out all the others on the evening of the 20th of September, exactly resembled Forster."

So the murderer was caught easily enough; it could hardly have been easier if he had given himself up.

Now comes one of the oddest parts of the case:

"As soon as the prisoners reached Nürnberg, at about

4 p.m. of the 24th, they were conducted, according to legal practice, to view the bodies lying in Bäumler's house. The corpses were laid in their coffins, with the faces exposed and the bodies covered with their own bloody garments; Bäumler on the right, and the maid-servant on the left hand, thus leaving a passage open between the coffins.

Paul Forster was brought in first: he stepped into the room, and between the two corpses, without the slightest change of countenance. When desired to look at them, he gazed steadfastly and coldly upon them, and replied to the question whether he knew the body on the right, 'No, I know it not; it is quite disfigured: I know it not.' And to the second question, 'Do you know this one to the left?' he answered in the same manner, 'No, she has lain in the grave; I know her not.' When asked how he knew that the body had lain in the grave, he replied, pointing to the face, 'Because she is so disfigured; the face is quite decayed here!' On being desired by the judge to point out the exact spot which he thought so decayed, with a constrained air, but with the coarsest indifference, he grasped the head of the murdered woman, pressed the brow, the broken nose, and the cheeks with his fingers, and said quite coolly, 'Here: you may see it clearly!' He attempted to evade every question addressed to him by the judge, by affecting that the idea of murder was so utterly foreign to him, that in all innocence and simplicity he mistook the deadly wounds for the result of decay.

All the endeavours of the judge to wring some sign of embarrassment or feeling from this man, as he stood between his two victims, were vain: his iron soul was unmoved. Only once, when asked, 'Where, then, is the corn-chandler to whom the house belongs?' he appeared staggered, but only for a moment. The judge went so far in his zeal, as to desire him to hold the hands of both corpses, and then to say what he felt. Without a moment's hesitation, Forster grasped the cold hand of Bäumler in his right, and that of Schütz in his left hand;

and answered, 'He feels cold – ah, she is cold too;' an answer which clearly contained a sort of contemptuous sneer at the judge's question. During the whole scene, the tone of his voice was as soft and sanctimonious, and his manner as calm, as his feelings were cold and unmoved.

His mistress's behaviour was very different: she was much shaken on entering the room. When desired to look at the dead bodies, she did so, but instantly turned away shuddering, and asked for water. She declared that she knew nothing of these persons, or of the manner of their death. She said that she had learned that she was supposed to be implicated in the horrible deed from the populace, who crowded in thousands round the carriage which brought them from Fürth to Nürnberg, calling her a murderess, striking her with their fists and sticks, and ill-using her in every way. But that God would manifest her innocence, and that she could bring witnesses to prove that she had not left her home at Diesbeck for some weeks. Her evident compassion for the victims, and horror of the crime, spoke more in favour of her innocence than her tears and protestations. An alibi was subsequently most clearly proved."

This method of getting the suspected murderer to view – and even touch – the corpse was common all over Europe at this period. Feuerbach comments that in cases of infanticide, this has never been known to fail. But this murderer was a hardened criminal, and was unaffected.

It was, of course, an open-and-shut case. The police were able to prove that Forster's sister had given him the axe with which he killed Bäumler and the maidservant. Forster continued to deny knowing anything about the murders until he saw that all these denials would only make things worse. So at this stage he changed his story, and explained that the murders had actually been committed by two men called Schlemmer, who had offered to take him with them to Bohemia, where their rich relations would give him a job. He had met them later in the day, and they had offered to look after his axe while he took a letter to the post. They then vanished with his axe. He met them later at the brandy shop, after all the other guests had gone, and they sent him to go and look out for their cart, which was due to arrive about ten. While he was still waiting for the cart, the Schlemmer's joined him, carrying a trunk and a white parcel. The cart now arrived, and they drove off to the city gate, where the Schlemmer's told him they would not take him to Bohemia after all, but would give him a present . . . This was the white parcel, and when Forster got it home, he found that it contained some bloodstained clothes, and the bags of money that were found in his mistress's house.

It was an absurd story, but the judges had to check it out. They suspected, in any case, that Forster had had accomplices, because Bäumler was reputed to be a very rich man, and should have had far more than the 350 or so florins found in Forster's possession. They checked – with German thoroughness – but finally concluded that the Schlemmer's were a figment of Forster's imagination.

Still Forster fought every inch of the way. He had good reason: a man could not be executed unless he confessed. And by 1820, torture had been abolished in Bavaria. (Feuerbach had been responsible for that, in 1806.) Eventually, he was found guilty, and sentenced to life imprisonment in chains, with hard labour. His sister was sentenced to a year in prison as an accomplice.

And that seems to be the end of the case. But in fact, the most interesting part is still to come. Feuerbach goes on to quote at length from an autobiography written by Forster when he was in jail for burglary two years earlier. And this makes it clear that Forster was far from being a brutal and basically stupid killer. He calls it *The Romance of My Life and Loves*, and even Feuerbach is compelled to admit that parts are very well written indeed.

John Paul Forster explains that as a child, he was quiet and thoughtful. A baron came to live in a house in which Forster's father was the gardener, and Forster got to know the baron's two children, and greatly enjoyed acting as a kind of servant to them. The baron liked this so much that he used to invite Forster over every day. His schoolfriends and even his brother began to call him a snob, and refused to play with him. But John Paul had glimpsed a way of life that filled him with longing. And when he left school, the baron offered him a job as a servant. He dressed in grey livery, and accompanied his master and mistress

to "balls and assemblies". He was in the seventh heaven, says
Feuerbach.

Then came the blow that would eventually turn Forster into
a criminal. His father, who was religious, decided that John
Paul ought to become a shoemaker. John Paul flatly refused;
but he finally agreed to learn the trade of gardening, because
that gave him an opportunity of "coming into contact with
gentlefolks". And he was apparently an excellent gardener –
until he was conscripted into the army (This was about 1805,
when all Europe was in arms against Napoleon.)

From then on, things went from bad to worse. He hated army
life, with its beatings and semi-starvation. (Again, we have to
remember that soldiers were beaten as a matter of course.) He
was always in trouble with the NCOs, always being flogged or
thrown into jail. One day he stole away to spend the night with
a cook named Babetta, with whom he was in love; he returned
the next day, but his absence had been noted, and he received
twenty lashes.

In 1810 he fell in love again, this time with Margaretha Preiss.
He badly wanted to leave the army, but was not allowed to. He
began trying to get himself thrown out of the army by thieving.
He also deserted several times, and was sentenced each time
to "run the gauntlet" (which was as painful as being flogged)
and sentenced to serve another six years in the army. Finally,
his crimes caused so much trouble that he was drummed out
in disgrace.

That, of course, was what he wanted; but ten years of
cheating, lying and deserting had undermined his character,
and made him bitter. He was soon in jail for three and a half
years for burglary. There he wrote the autobiography, intended
as a legacy for his beloved Margaretha. Feuerbach sneers that it
illustrates how important he thought he was, and quotes with
contempt passages about the "soft murmuring of the evening
breezes and the melting harmony of the senses." In fact, they
reveal that Forster was genuinely a tragic "outsider" figure, a
man who had had a glimpse of freedom and then had it snatched
from him. The amount of poetry that he quotes reveals that he
was highly literate.

The murder, admittedly, was utterly stupid, the act of a
man who wanted to get rich quick and marry his Margaretha.
Like Raskolnikov in Dostoevsky's *Crime and Punishment*, he was

hoping that one single crime would bring him thousands of florins, enough to give him a start in life. Instead, he was to spend the rest of his life in chains. But even the account of his years in jail make us aware that he was no common criminal. Feuerbach says: "For years Forster had borne in dogged silence the hardships of imprisonment, the misery of civil death, the burden of his chains, and the still heavier burden of a troubled conscience." All attempts to make him confess were a failure. His life was totally ruined, yet he told his fellow prisoners: "Steadfastness of purpose is the chief ornament of a man. He should not easily give up life; however wretched, life is a noble thing. Believe me, comrades, whenever I look upon my ball and chain, I feel proud to think that even on my death bed my last breath shall be drawn with courage." He even polished his chains until they "shone like silver". At first he used to enthrall his fellow prisoners – who all regarded him with the deepest respect – with amazing stories "of enchanted princes and princesses"; then he suddenly decided to speak only in monosyllables, and kept up this resolution "out of pride" for the rest of his life (or what we know of the rest of it.)

His stubbornness was unbending. When given work he considered too hard for him he refused to do it. He was lashed, "receiving the severest blows without moving a muscle or uttering a sound, and returned to his cell just as if nothing had happened." He was beaten again and again, each time he refused to do the work; at last the authorities were forced to give way, and allow him to do the work he preferred.

Feuerbach ends his account by telling us that Forster's face is "vulgar and heavy", the lower part so long that it gives him the look of an animal. Although a humanitarian, he obviously regards John Paul Forster as a contemptible ruffian. For the modern reader, Forster's story is one of tragically wasted powers. He had "ideas above his station", and he had the kind of courage and determination that might have brought him fame and success. Instead, he spent the rest of his life – he was still alive when Feuerbach described the case – mouldering in Lichtenau jail. Life in the year 1820 could be devastatingly cruel.

Anna Zwanziger

The same point is made by Feuerbach's most remarkable story: his account of the mass poisoner Anna Zwanziger. Again, I quote his account of her crimes:

"In the year 1807 a widow, nearly fifty years of age, calling herself Nanette Schönleben, lived at Pegnitz in the territory of Baireuth, supporting herself by knitting. Her conduct gained her a reputation which induced Justice Wolfgang Glaser, who was then living at Rosendorf separated from his wife, to take her as his housekeeper, on the 5th March, 1808. On the 22nd of the following July Glaser was reconciled to his wife, who had been living with her relations at Grieshaber near Augsburg. Soon after her return to her husband's house, though a strong healthy woman, she was suddenly seized with violent vomiting, diarrhœa, &c., and on the 26th August, a month after the reconciliation, she died.

Anna Schönleben now left Glaser's service, and on the 25th September she went to live as house-keeper with Justice Grohmann at Sanspareil. Her new master, who was unmarried, was thirty-eight years of age, and though a large and powerful man, had suffered from gout for several years, and was often confined to his bed. On these occasions Anna Schönleben always nursed him with the utmost care. In the spring of 1809 he was seized with an illness more violent than any he had had before, and accompanied by entirely new symptoms, – violent vomiting, pains in the stomach, diarrhœa, heat and dryness of the skin, inflammation of the mouth and throat, insatiable thirst, and excessive weakness and pains in the limbs. He died on the 8th May, after an illness of eleven days, and his housekeeper appeared inconsolable for his loss. Every one, the medical men included, took it for granted that Grohmann, who had long been ailing, had died a natural death.

Anna Schönleben was once more out of place, but her reputation for kindness, activity, attention and skill as a sick-nurse soon procured her a new home. At the time of Grohmann's death the wife of the magistrate Gebhard was just expecting to be brought to bed, and asked Anna Schönleben to attend her as nurse and housekeeper during her lying-in. Anna Schönleben, always willing to oblige, readily agreed, and from the day of the confinement she resided in Gebhard's house, dividing her time between the care of the household and of the child. Madame Gebhard was confined on the 13th May, 1809, and both the mother and the child were doing very well until the third day, which the mother fell ill. Her illness became more alarming every day; she was seized with violent vomiting, nervous agitation, distressing heat in the intestines, inflammation in the throat, &c.; and on the 20th May, seven days after her confinement, she died, exclaiming in her agony, 'Merciful Heaven! you have given me poison!' As Madame Gebhard had always been sickly, and moreover had died in childbirth, her death excited no suspicion, and, like Madame Glaser and Grohmann, she was buried without more ado. The widower, embarrassed by his household and the infant which was left upon his hands, thought that he could do nothing better than to keep Anna Schönleben as his housekeeper. Several persons endeavoured to change his resolution. They said that this woman carried death with her wherever she went; that three young persons whom she had served, had died one after the other within a very short time. No one made the smallest accusation against her; their warnings arose from a mere superstitions dread of an unfortunate sympathetic influence exercised by her upon those with whom she lived: her obliging deportment, her piety, and her air of honesty, humility and kindness, protected her from every breath of suspicion. Thus she remained for several months in Gebhard's service unsuspected and unaccused.

During her residence in Gebhard's house various

suspicious events occurred, without, however, exciting attention. On the 25th August, 1809, a certain Beck, and the widow Alberti, dined with Gebhard. Soon after dinner they were both seized with violent vomiting, colic, spasms, &c., which lasted until late at night. About the same time she gave the messenger Rosenhauer a glass of white wine, and not long after he had swallowed it he was attacked in precisely the same manner, and was so ill as to be forced to go to bed. On the very same day she took Rosenhauer's porter, a lad of nineteen named Johann Kraus, into the cellar and gave him a glass of brandy. After drinking a small quantity he perceived a sort of white sediment in it, and therefore left the rest, but in a short time he felt very sick. During the last week of August, one of Gebhard's maid-servants, Barbara Waldmann, with whom Anna Schönleben had had several trifling disputes, was taken ill after drinking a cup of coffee, and vomited every half-hour during the whole day. The most remarkable occurrence, however, took place on the 1st September. Gebhard, while playing at skittles with a party of his friends, sent for a few pitchers of beer from his own cellar. He and five other persons drank some of the beer, and were seized soon after with sickness and internal pains; some of the party, among whom was Gebhard, were so ill as to require medical aid.

This first inspired distrust and dislike of Anna Schönleben. On the following day, chiefly at the instigation of one of his fellow-sufferers at the skittle-ground, Gebhard dismissed her from his service, but gave her a written character for honesty and fidelity.

She was to leave Sanspareil for Baireuth on the next day – 3rd September. She expressed her surprise at so sudden a dismissal, but was civil and obliging as usual, and busied herself during the whole evening in various domestic arrangements. Among other things she took the salt-box out of the kitchen (which was no part of her usual duty), and filled it from a barrel of salt which stood in Gebhard's bedroom. When the maid-servant Waldmann commented upon this, Anna Schönleben said, in a jesting manner, that she must do so, for that if those who were going away filled the salt-box, the other servants would keep their places the longer. On the morning of her departure she affected the greatest friendship for the two maid-servants, Hazin and Waldmann, and gave each of them a cup of coffee sweetened with sugar which she took out of a piece of paper. While the carriage was waiting for her at the door she took Gebhard's child, an infant five months old, in her arms, gave it a biscuit soaked in milk to eat, then let it drink the milk, and finally parted from it with the most tender caresses, and got into the carriage which was to convey her to Baireuth, and which Gebhard paid for, besides giving her a crown dollar and some chocolate.

She had been gone scarce half an hour when the child became alarmingly ill and vomited terribly, and in a few hours more the two maid-servants were attacked in the same manner; and now, for the first time, suspicion was excited. On hearing from his servants how Anna Schönleben had busied herself, Gebhard had the contents of the kitchen salt-box analyzed by a chemist, and a large quantity of arsenic was found among it. The salt-barrel was likewise found at the trial to contain thirty grains of arsenic to every three pounds of salt."

Anna Zwanziger was caught fairly easily. After wandering around for a few months, hoping that Judge Gebhard would send for her – she was obviously slightly insane – she made the mistake of returning to Nuremberg, where she was arrested. Two packets of arsenic were found in her possession. The science of toxicology – detecting poisons – had recently made enormous strides, and when Frau Glaser's body was exhumed, large quantities of arsenic were found. Faced with this evidence, she finally confessed, and was executed by sword in 1811.

Once again, Feuerbach's account of her life throws an entirely new light on the case, and even if we end by feeling no sympathy for the mass murderess, we at least begin to understand why she did it. Born in Nuremberg in August, 1760, the daughter of an innkeeper, Anna was orphaned by the time she was five. After living for five years with various relatives, she was taken at the age of ten into the house of her guardian, a wealthy merchant, and there received a good education. She was more fortunate than John Paul Forster, for she actually lived the kind of life Forster only dreamed about. But when she was fifteen, her guardian decided to marry her to a drunken lawyer named Zwanziger, who was more than twice her age. She objected, but finally had to give way.

Spending most of her days alone, while her husband was out drinking with cronies, she became an avid reader of novels and plays. She was so moved by Goethe's *Sorrows of Young Werther* – which had caused an epidemic of suicide ten years earlier – that she was also tempted to kill herself. She also read Richardson's novel *Pamela*, about a servant girl whose master tries hard to seduce her, but is finally so overcome by her virtue and goodness that he marries her. This also exercised a powerful influence on her. And she was deeply moved by Lessing's tragedy *Emilia Galeotti*, about a girl who is pursued by a wicked prince (who has murdered her fiancée) and ends by persuading her father to kill her to prevent rape.

Her husband soon spent her inheritance – he was capable of drinking ten bottles of wine a day, and was soon a hopeless alcoholic. Anna was now forced to become a high class prostitute to support her husband and two children – although she claimed she only slept with gentlemen. This, at least, was better than starving; she learned to use her physical charms to persuade men to support her. She even thought up a brilliant scheme involving a lottery of watches (we would call it a raffle), which

---

James Marsh, the British chemist who invented an incredibly sensitive test for arsenic – so sensitive that it could detect a thousandth of a milligram of arsenic – was a scientific prodigy who was never appreciated. He worked all his life for thirty shillings a week at the Royal Military Academy. For his great discovery he was given the gold medal of the Society of Arts – but would have undoubtedly preferred cash. Frustration turned him into an alcoholic and when he died at 52, he left his wife and children destitute.

once again made them prosperous; but her husband again spent the money. One lover, a lieutenant, persuaded her to leave her husband, but her husband then persuaded her to return. When she divorced him, he persuaded her to remarry him the next day. Clearly, Anna was not the ruthless bitch Feuerbach represents her as. She admits that she ended by feeling very fond of him.

Finally, Zwanziger died, and after eighteen years, Anna was left on her own. There was no national assistance or social security in Bavaria in 1796. she had to find a way to support herself and her children. She tried to set up a sweetshop in Vienna, but it failed. She became a housekeeper, but had to leave when she had an illegitimate child by a clerk – she put it into a foundling's home, where it died.

Anna was now thirty-eight, still attractive to men. She found a "protector" who installed her in lodgings, and tried to supplement her income with doll making. Tired of being a kept woman, she accepted an excellent job as a housekeeper in the home of a minister, but left after a few months – Feuerbach says because of her dirty habits, but more probably because she gave herself "airs and graces". For, as Feuerbach remarks perceptively, "the insupportable thought of having fallen from her station as mistress of a house and family to the condition of a servant, worked so strongly on her feelings as to cause her to behave like a madwoman." In short, the ups and downs of her life caused her to suffer a mental breakdown. "She laughed, wept and prayed by turns. She received her mistress's orders with a laugh, and went obediently away, but never executed them."

Anna was now definitely insane, and in her misery, she retained one basic obsession: to have a man to look after her and protect her. But her physical charms were fast disappearing. Her old "protector" took her back for a while and got her pregnant again, then left her to chase an actress. She had a miscarriage. After that she attempted suicide by drowning, but was rescued by two fishermen. She was ill with fever for several weeks.

At the age of forty-four, no longer attractive, Anna was forced to take an ill-paid job as a housemaid; now she was at a kind of rock bottom. She stole a diamond ring and absconded. Her master reacted by placing a notice in the newspapers naming her as a thief, which destroyed any remnants of reputation she still possessed. Her son-in-law, with whom she was staying, threw her out.

In the following year, it looked as if fate had finally smiled on her. Working as a needlework teacher, she attracted an old general and became his mistress. Again she dreamed of security and being in charge of her own household. But he walked out on her, and ignored her letters.

And so, in 1807, after more miserable wandering from place to place, she found herself in Pegnitz, near Baireuth, where she was offered a job by Judge Glaser. (To explain her preference for judges, we have to remember that her first husband was a lawyer.) At fifty, the craving for security had given her the cunning of a madwoman. She poisoned the wife of Judge Glaser, hoping he would marry her – an insane hope, since she was now skinny, sallow and ugly. She moved on to the home of Judge Grohmann, who was unmarried and twelve years her junior. Now, surely, she had found the man who was destined to bring security to her old age . . .? Grohmann suffered from gout, and she enjoyed nursing him. She enjoyed nursing him so much that she began slipping small quantities of arsenic and antimony into his food. Eventually, she overdid it – this seems clear, since she can have had no reason to kill her meal ticket – and he died. Feuerbach says she appeared inconsolable, and this is almost certainly because she was.

And so it continued – the tragedy of a madwoman who remembered that she had once been a mistress with servants, an attractive women whom men had once desired, and who was now incapable of facing reality. In our own society, she would have been confined in an asylum after her trial, and so found some kind of security in her final years. As it was, she knelt down at the block, and her head fell into the headsman's basket. Perhaps the woman who had identified with Emilia Galeotti and Pamela felt that it was more appropriate than dying in a workhouse.

Andrew Bichel

Feuerbach records another case of a multiple killer that has the odd distinction of being possibly the first recorded instance of what we would now call the sex murder. This statement must immediately be qualified by saying that there have always been sex crimes, particularly during wars, and that the sixteen century Nuremberg executioner Hans Schmidt records a number of cases in which robbers have also raped their female victims. But the sex crimes of the past were usually committed by drunks, or (as in the case of Schmidt's robbers) with rape as the secondary aim. Bichel's crimes seem to have been motivated by some odd sexual perversion which was certainly not understood at the time.

The case was discussed by Major Arthur Griffiths, one of the best of the late nineteenth century historians of crime, whose *Mysteries of Police and Crime*, published in 1898, is still highly readable. Here is his description of the Bichel case.

"One of the earliest cases recorded is that of Andrew Bichel, who lived at Regendorf, in Bavaria. His character was strangely contradictory. Until his terrible misdeeds were finally brought home to him, he did not enjoy a bad reputation. He was not a drunkard, nor a gambler, nor quarrelsome; he was married to a wife with whom he lived on good terms, had children, and was esteemed for his piety. But below the surface he was a pilferer and petty thief; suspected of robbing his neighbours' gardens, he was caught by the master he served, an inn-keeper of Regendorf, stealing hay from his loft. His nature really was abjectly and inordinately covetous; he was a coward who persisted in his crimes because he seemed to have secured perfect immunity from detection. They were committed on the defenceless; his victims were helpless, credulous women, who trusted him and made no attempt to defend themselves. Cunning in him was allied to great cruelty, and both were backed by such extraordinary greed that he thought the pettiest plunder worth the greatest crime. 'A man thus constituted will commit no crimes requiring energy or courage,' writes the judge who tried him. 'He will never venture to rob on the highway, or break into a house; but he would commit arson, administer poison, murder a man in his sleep, or, like Bichel, cunningly induce young girls to go to him, and then murder them in cold blood for the sake of their clothes or a few pence.'

No suspicion was roused against Bichel for years. Girls went to Regendorf, and were never heard of again. One, Barbara Reisinger, disappeared in 1807, and another, Catherine Seidel, the year after. In both cases no report was made to the police until a long time had elapsed, and a first clue to the disappearance of the last-named was obtained by a sister, who found a tailor making up a waistcoat from a piece of dimity which she recognised as having formed part of a petticoat worn by Catherine when she was last seen. The waistcoat was for a certain Andrew Bichel, who lived in the town, and who now followed the curious profession of fortune-teller.

Catherine Seidel had been attracted by his promises to show her fortune in a glass. She was to come to him in her best clothes, the best she had, and with three changes, for this was part of the performance. She went as directed, and was never heard of again. Bichel, when asked, declared she had eloped with a man she met at his house.

Now that suspicion was aroused against Bichel, his house in Regendorf was searched, and a chest full of women's clothes was found in his room. Among them were many garments identified as belonging to the missing Catherine Seidel. One of her handkerchiefs, moreover, was taken out of his pocket when he was apprehended.

Still there was no direct proof of murder. The disappearance of Seidel was undoubted, Reisinger's also, and the presumption of foul play was strong. Some crime had been committed, but whether abduction, manslaughter, or murder was still a hidden mystery.

Repeated searchings of Bichel's house were fruitless;
no dead bodies were found, no stains of blood, no
traces of violence.

The dog of a police sergeant first ran the crime to
ground. He pointed so constantly to a wood-shed in
the yard, and when called off so persistently returned
to the same spot, that the officer determined to
explore the shed thoroughly. In one corner lay a
great heap of straw and litter, and on digging deep
below this they turned up a quantity of human bones.
They went a foot deeper, and found more remains.
Near at hand, underneath a pile of logs by a chalk pit,
a human head was found. Not far off was a second
body, which, like the first, had been cut in half. One
was believed to be the corpse of Barbara Reisinger,
the other was actually identified, through a pair of
pinchbeck earrings, as that of Catherine Seidel.

Bichel stood defiant before the searching questions
of the judge; he lied continually, and was proved to
have lied. Still he would make no avowal. Even when
confronted with the corpses of his alleged victims,
as was then the custom in Bavaria, he would not
yield. Although so greatly agitated that he all but
fainted on the spot, he had yet the strength of will
to master his emotions, and when again asked if he
recognised his handiwork, he protested that he had
never seen the corpses before. 'I only trembled,' he
protested, when taxed with the weakness, 'I only
trembled at the sight. Who would not tremble on
such an occasion?' But he could not stand; he sank
into a chair. All his muscles quivered; his face was
horribly contorted.

Yet a deep impression had been left on his mind,
and when relegated to prison 'his imagination,'
as Feuerbach says, 'overcame his obstinacy.' He
made full confession of these two particular crimes.
Reisinger he had killed when she came seeking a
situation as maid-servant. He was tempted by her
clothes. To murder he had recourse to his trade
of fortune-telling, saying he would show her in
a magic mirror her future fate, and producing a

board and a small magnifying glass, placed them on a table in front of her. She must not touch these sacred objects; her eyes must be bandaged, her hands tied behind her back. No sooner had she consented than he stabbed her in the neck, and it was all over with her.

This success emboldened him to repeat the operation. He sought to entrap other girls, choosing always the best dressed, and putting forward the bait of the magic mirror. But he failed with three, and then caught Catherine Seidel in the toils. The process was exactly the same as with Barbara Reisinger, but this victim was not killed so easily. The after part was the same.

Bichel now resolved to adopt murder as a trade, and looked about him for fresh victims. But although the motive was strong and his cunning great, he does not seem to have enticed many more within reach of his knife. The police heard of several cases in which he had used the same lure of the magic glass upon girls who promised to go to him dressed in their best, but who, fortunately for themselves, thought better of it. They escaped, some by want of faith in the mirror, others by a secret aversion to Bichel, a few by mere accident.

Bichel, was found guilty and condemned to be broken on the wheel, but the sentence was commuted to beheading."

Why did Bichel murder girls? Feuerbach seems to accept Bichel's own explanation. "My only reason for murdering Reisinger and Seidel was desire for their clothes." But the next sentence contradicts this. "I must confess I did not want them; but it was exactly as if someone stood at my elbow and whispered: "Do this and buy corn." Which makes it sound as if Bichel's extreme poverty drove him to crime. But if that *was* his motive, then why did he keep the clothes?

A modern psychiatrist would have interviewed Bichel until he understood his motives. Was he, perhaps, fascinated by his sister's clothes as a child, and enjoyed dressing up in them? Did he have some deep resentment of well-dressed women that aroused a kind of sadistic desire to kill? Or is it possible that the motive was simply rape? At this distance in time, we shall never know. And unfortunately, Feuerbach himself has failed to provide us with the biographical clues that he unearthed in the case of Forster and Anna Zwanziger . . .

• chapter three •

NOTORIOUS AMERICAN CASES

C riminally speaking, America in the early nineteenth century is relatively uninteresting. There were plenty of violent deaths, of course, but they were mostly the work of bandits and common criminals. Soon after World War II, a New York publisher issued a series of volumes on murders in major cities – New York murders, Chicago murders, Denver murders, and so on.
But few of them contain any cases before 1850.

The same applies to the best compilation of American crime in the nineteenth century, Thomas S. Duke's Celebrated Criminal Cases of America, published in San Francisco in 1910. The book is full of marvellous accounts of riots and robberies and Indian massacres, of political assassins and murderous thugs. But there are few cases that rate as criminological classics, on the level of Burke and Hare or Lacenaire or Anna Zwanziger.

One of the rare exceptions is the amazing story of the murder in the Harvard Medical School. Thomas Duke was an ex-policeman, and his down-to-earth, factual way of telling the story adds to its impact.

In North Carolina, Lavinia Fisher has become a legend, like Calamity Jane or Bonnie Parker. Lavinia and her husband John Fisher were members of a gang of highwaymen who, in 1818, operated from Six Mile House, north of Charleston, and robbed passing travellers. Cavalry surrounded the house and ordered the gang to leave. They did so quietly, and the cavalry left behind a young man called David Ross to guard the house. The next day the gang came back and threw him out; the beautiful Lavinia attacked him and pushed his head through a pane of glass. The enraged lawmen returned and forced the gang to surrender. Most of them were sentenced to death for highway robbery. But Lavinia persuaded the susceptible prison governor to allow them to occupy a more comfortable – and less secure – part of the jail. In September 1818, they knocked a hole in the wall, and John Fisher and some others escaped down a rope made of sheets. But the rope broke before Lavinia could follow, and John refused to escape without her. Although they received one reprieve, both met the hangman in February 1819, Lavinia fighting and screaming to the last. She seems to have been a bad tempered termagant – but to the people of Charleston she is still the beautiful highwaywoman who went to her death without flinching.

Professor Webster

"On Friday, November 23, 1849, one of the most prominent physicians in Boston, Dr George Parkman, mysteriously disappeared. Being very methodical in his habits, his family immediately suspected foul play.

He was the owner of many tenement houses and was rather exacting in his attitude toward his tenants, many of whom were of the rougher class. As he collected the rents himself, the authorities proceeded on the theory that he had antagonized some of these tenants to such an extent that they murdered him for the double purpose of revenge and robbery, and then concealed his body.

The river was dredged and the doctor's tenements and the buildings adjacent thereto were thoroughly searched, but no trace was found of the missing man, although large rewards were offered.

When the doctor left home, about noon on November 23, he stated that he had an appointment with a person at 2:30 p.m., but did not divulge the name of the person.

About 1:30 p.m. he entered the grocery store conducted by Paul Holland, at Vine and Blossom streets, and after leaving an order, he asked permission to leave a paper bag containing a head of lettuce at the store for a few moments, but he never returned for it. This grocery store was but a short distance from one of the leading medical colleges in Boston, the college being located on Grove street. Elias Fuller, who conducted an iron foundry adjacent to the medical college, and his brother, Albert, saw Dr Parkman in front of the college about 2 p.m. on the date of his disappearance.

Dr John Webster was the professor of chemistry at this college and also at Harvard College. His standing in the social and professional world was equal to that of Dr Parkman, and their families were on terms of considerable intimacy.

Notwithstanding the fact that Dr Parkman called on Dr Webster at the college at 2 p.m. on Friday, the 23rd instant, and his subsequent disappearance was the principal topic of conversation in Boston the next day and for some time afterward, Dr Webster did not inform the almost distracted members of the Parkman family of this visit until the Sunday evening following, although it was proven that he saw an account of the doctor's disappearance in the Boston Transcript on Saturday afternoon.

Dr Webster then stated that Dr Parkman called on him for the purpose of collecting $450 which Webster had previously borrowed, giving as security a mortgage on a piece of real estate.

He claimed that he paid Dr Parkman the full amount due, from the proceeds of the sale of tickets to his course of lectures in the college.

Dr Parkman held a note for this amount, which he

had in his possession when he called on Dr Webster
and which the latter subsequently produced to prove
that he had paid the money. He added that Dr
Parkman stated that he would proceed forthwith to
Cambridge and cancel the mortgage.

Dr Webster also claimed that he saw Dr Parkman
go down stairs and leave the college after this
transaction.

Webster made many conflicting statements as to
the denomination of the money paid and as to the
circumstances under which it was paid, but his
standing in the community was such that it was
difficult to believe him guilty of any wrong-doing
and it would have been considered preposterous at
that time to even suspect him of being implicated in
the murder of his friend and benefactor.

Merely as a matter of form, the authorities decided
to search the medical college, but before proceeding
with the formal search an apology was made to Dr
Webster for the intrusion.

When Ephraim Littlefield, the janitor of the building, observed the farcical search, he looked on with
disapproving eyes, and intimated that a more thor-
ough search would result in sensational discoveries.

The authorities then questioned Littlefield closely,
and he made the following statement:

"I have known Dr Parkman for many years. On
Monday evening, November 19, 1849, I was assisting
Dr Webster when Dr Parkman entered the room. He
appeared to be angry at Dr Webster and without any
preliminary conversation, abruptly said: 'Dr Webster,
are you ready for me tonight?'

"Webster replied, 'No, I am not, doctor.'

"I then moved away, but I heard Dr Parkman
reprimand him for selling mortgaged property, and
in a final burst of anger said: 'Something must be
done to-morrow,' and he then left.

"On the morning of Friday, November 23, I saw
a sledge hammer which belonged in the laboratory,
behind Dr Webster's door. I had never seen it there
before and have been unable to find it since.

"At 2:15 p.m. I was at the front door and saw Dr Parkman approaching the college, but I went inside and did not see him enter the building. About one hour afterward I went to Dr Webster's laboratory to clean up, but found the door bolted from the inside.

"I knocked loudly but received no response, although I heard someone walking inside who, I supposed, was Dr Webster. I then tried all the different doors leading to his laboratory, but they were all locked from the inside – a most unusual occurrence.

"At 4 o'clock I tried the doors again, with the same result. At 5 p.m. I saw Dr Webster leave the building from the back exit.

"I went to a party that night, and at 11 p.m. returned to the college, where my wife and I are domiciled. I again tried Dr Webster's door and again found it locked.

"On the next day, Saturday, Dr Webster was in his laboratory all day, but I did not go near him. That evening I met him on the street, and we discussed the article in the evening paper about the disappearance of Dr Parkman.

"Formerly he would look me in the face when talking, but on this occasion he hung his head and was pale and agitated. On Sunday and Monday the doors to the laboratory were still locked. On Tuesday I found the doctor's room open and mentioned the fact to my wife.

"On this day he was exceptionally friendly toward me and gave me an order for a Thanksgiving turkey. This was remarkable, as I had known him for eight years, and it was the first time I ever knew of him giving anything away.

"On Wednesday, Dr Webster came to the college early and again locked the door.

"The flue from his furnace is between the walls near the stairs leading to the demonstrator's room, and when I passed up the stairs the wall was extremely hot."

The janitor's statement in regard to the door to the

laboratory being constantly locked for several days subsequent to the disappearance of Dr Parkman was corroborated by several persons who had called during that period.

These disclosures were made on Thursday, November 29, and the officers proceeded at once to Dr Webster's laboratory, and after vigorous knocking, the door was unbolted from the inside and the officers were admitted by Dr Webster, but nothing was said regarding the janitor's statement.

At this time a bright fire was burning in the furnace. Nothing was found on this date, and the search was resumed on Friday in the absence of Dr Webster.

In the meantime the furnace had become cool enough to permit of an examination, which resulted in the finding of a fractured skull containing a full set of mineral teeth.

By means of a trap door, the officers descended to the cellar, where they found a right leg.

In a tea chest they found the upper part of a man's body and the left leg. The shape of the body corresponded with that of Dr Parkman.

Dr Winslow Lewis and two other reputable surgeons stated that the manner in which the body was separated indicated that it was done by someone having knowledge of anatomy.

The fact that these remains were found concealed in the chemical laboratory where no such subjects were required, made it apparent that they were the remains of some victim of foul play, and Dr Ainsworth, the demonstrator of anatomy at the college, stated that they were not parts of any subject used in the college for dissection.

Dr N. C. Keep, who had made a full set of false teeth for Dr Parkman, inspected the plate and teeth and identified them as work he had done for Dr Parkman, because of a peculiarity of the lower jaw, which caused him much trouble. But to be positive, he produced the model, which fitted the plates exactly.

The result of the police investigations were not

made public until it was proven beyond all doubt that the remains of Dr Parkman had been found. Police Officer Clapp was then sent to Dr Webster's home at Cambridge to arrest him for murder.

When the public learned of the arrest of the eminent professor, it was at once concluded that a grave mistake had been made and that too much credence had been given to the statement of the janitor, who possibly was attempting to shield himself.

At the trial it was proven that notwithstanding his outward show of prosperity, Dr Webster was financially embarrassed. It was proven that he had committed a felony by selling the property upon which Dr Parkman held a mortgage for $450 and that the latter threatened to prosecute him for this offense if he did not immediately pay the principal and interest, amounting to $483.60.

It was proven that it was utterly impossible for Dr Webster, who saw the state prison and ruin staring him in the face, to raise this small amount of money.

It was proven that he lied when he stated that he paid this amount from the proceeds of the sale of tickets to his course of lectures at the college, as he had received no such amount, and a large portion of what he *did* receive was paid to others.

It was proven that Dr Webster called at Dr Parkman's house and requested the latter to call at the college at 2:30 p.m. on November 23 for the purpose of making a final settlement.

Dr Webster could give no reason for keeping a roaring fire in the furnace for several days after Dr Parkman's disappearance, and during the Thanksgiving holidays, when all of the other professors were enjoying a week of recreation.

While it was the duty of the janitor to build the fires, the latter was barred from Dr Webster's apartments, who personally attended to the building and feeding of the fire.

It was proven that the upper part of the body and left leg found in the tea chest were tied together by a peculiar kind of twine and that Dr Webster had, on November 27, purchased similar twine and several fish hooks which were found in his apartments.

It was proven that when the officers approached the room in which the tea chest containing a greater part of the body was found, Dr Webster endeavored to discourage them from searching that room by stating that highly explosive chemicals were stored there.

A pair of trousers belonging to Dr Webster was found in a closet and subjected to a microscopical examination with the result that human blood was found.

While the search was being made for Dr Parkman, the City Marshal of Boston received three anonymous letters.

One, supposed to have been written by an illiterate person, suggested that a search be made on "brooklynt heights," another stated that Dr Parkman had gone to sea on the ship "Herculian," and a third, signed "Civis," stated positively that the missing doctor had been seen at Cambridge.

Handwriting experts swore positively that all three letters were written by Dr Webster.

The defense produced witnesses to prove the previous good character of Dr Webster and also introduced testimony to the effect that Dr Parkman had been seen after the defendant claimed he left the college. After producing medical experts to contradict the medical testimony introduced by the prosecution, the case was submitted.

Chief Justice Shaw then delivered his charge to the jury, and his instructions regarding circumstantial evidence were so able, comprehensive, and discriminating that they have since been regarded as a model by many of the leading jurists of America. When the cause was finally submitted to the jurors, they almost immediately agreed that the defendant was guilty. As Justice Shaw was also officially connected with Harvard College and had been friendly with Dr Webster for years, he almost collapsed while pronouncing the death penalty on his erstwhile friend.

The date of execution was set for August 30, 1850. Notwithstanding efforts made to obtain executive clemency, Dr Webster went to the gallows on that day, publicly protesting his innocence, although it was claimed that he confessed his guilt to a clergyman."

The Bender Family

London's legendary Sweeney Todd, the Demon Barber of Fleet Street, who precipitated customers into the basement from a swivelling barber's chair, then cut their throats, never existed except in the imagination of his creator, the playwright George Dibdin Pitt. But thirty years after the first production of that famous play in 1842, a real American family, the Benders, achieved a gruesome notoriety that rivals that of the Demon Barber.

On 9 March, 1873, Dr William York left his brother's house in Fort Scott, Kansas to return home on horseback. Fort Scott

The most famous murder in American history took place literally by gaslight. As Abraham Lincoln sat in Ford's Theater in Washington on the night of 14 April, 1865, a 26-year-old actor named John Wilkes Booth walked into Lincoln's box and shot him behind the left ear with a one-shot Derringer pistol. Then, shouting "*Sic semper tyrannis*" ("Ever thus to tyrants") he leapt on to the stage. Unfortunately, his spur caught in the curtain and he fell, fracturing his left shinbone. The injury slowed his escape back to the south, and twelve days later, he and fellow-conspirator David Herold were surrounded by Union soldiers in a barn in Virginia. When Booth refused to surrender, the barn was set on fire. Then a shot rang out, and Booth fell dead – whether he shot himself, or was killed by one of the soldiers, was never discovered with certainty.

marked the border of the Indian territories, but Dr York's journey was through safe, settled prairie and ought to have been uneventful. However Dr York did not arrive back in Independence, his home town. Weeks passed and nothing was heard from him. Something was evidently wrong. Colonel York, the doctor's brother, organized groups to search the area between Independence and Fort Scott. It was Colonel York himself who stopped at the Wayside Inn near Cherryvale to ask after his brother.

The inn was actually a tiny log cabin, roughly sixteen by twenty feet, surrounded by some farmland and an orchard. It was owned by European immigrants, the Bender family. The local people did not know exactly where they came from, only noticing that they spoke in thick guttural accents. The household consisted of Ma and Pa Bender, fifty and sixty respectively, and two grown-up children, both born in America. Kate Bender, the daughter, was a spiritualist and gave lectures on the subject as Professor Miss Kate Bender. She also advertised in the local paper as a faith healer who could not only cure disease, but also blindness and deafness. Their son was less gifted, only helping his father around the farm and inn. The whole family was heavily built and florid.

Colonel York knew that his brother had planned to stay at the Wayside Inn and thus made it one of the first places at which he enquired. Old Man Bender denied any knowledge of Dr York, pointing out that the Indians where still a real danger and that there were bandits everywhere. He and his son offered to help dredge the nearby river for Dr York's body. The Colonel was convinced and left to search elsewhere.

Soon another of the organized search parties called at the Benders' inn and asked after Dr York. Again they denied all, but after the party had left, they packed possessions into their covered wagon and fled.

No-one noticed they had gone for some while; guests were infrequent. Then on 9 May yet another search party noticed that the Wayside Inn seemed deserted, and that the cattle were making distressed noises. On entering, they found that the house stank of decomposition. At the back the cattle and sheep had been left penned for some time, and many were dead of thirst or hunger. Then someone noticed that the dry half-acre of orchard to the right of the house looked strange. The topsoil had been ploughed between the trees, and due to heavy rain some of the ploughed ground seemed to have subsided. The subsidence was in the shape of a grave.

Digging soon revealed the body of Dr York. His skull was crushed and his throat had been cut. Before nightfall seven other bodies had been recovered from the orchard's soil. All had been killed in the same way, except one small child who had been asphyxiated. From her position it seemed clear that she had been thrown into the grave alive, her murdered father thrown in on top of her, and both then covered over.

The next day another body of a child was unearthed. This one was so badly/decomposed that only its sex and approximate age could be ascertained. It was an eight-year-old girl. Unlike the other adult victims this girl seemed to have been deliberately mutilated, her right knee disconnected and her breastbone driven in.

Upon searching the inn, officers discovered that the smell was not only coming from the neglected animals. A trapdoor in the floor led down to a cellar – in fact a roughly-dug pit – coated in rancid blood.

The story behind the bodies soon emerged through deduction. The Bender family murdered guests who looked like they had some money. They would do this in an ingenious way. The dining area of the tiny cabin was divided from the sleeping area by a thick curtain suspended from the ceiling. The dining table was positioned within the small space in such a way as to make the diner sit with his back directly against the curtain. If the guest seemed worth the risk, either Old Man Bender or his son would wait in the sleeping area for a clear outline of the victim's head against the curtain and then smash the skull with a heavy stone-breaker's hammer. After searching the corpse for money, they would cut its throat in order to be certain that no life remained and then throw them down through the trapdoor in to the cellar to await nightfall and burial. The orchard turf was kept constantly ploughed in order to hide any signs of grave-digging.

Naturally the community of Cherryvale and its surroundings was horrified. Local farmers were quick to form a vigilante group and scour the area for signs of the Bender's flight. Four groups set out north, south, east and west to find their tracks. Another group "arrested" a Mr Brockman, an acquaintance of the Benders and an accomplice in the eyes of the local townsfolk because he had once been Bender's business partner. The vigilantes hanged him from a tree until he was almost dead in an attempt to force information from him.

Other local people began remembering strange events that at the time were ignored. A Mr Wetzell remembered answering Kate Bender's advert in the newspaper. He suffered from acute facial neuralgia, and decided to try Kate's mystic powers as a cure. He and a friend visited the inn, where Kate greeted them in a friendly and charming manner, telling him that she could easily cure his neuralgia, but would he not prefer some dinner first? The two guests sat down, whereupon Old Man Bender and his son, who had been watching them closely, disappeared behind the curtain. For a reason neither of them could adequately explain, the two guests decided to stand up and eat their dinner at the bar. At this Kate became angry and abusive, and the rest of the family looked on threateningly. Sensing that something strange was going on the two men quickly left.

Apart from this first-hand account of the Bender's methods, another piece of evidence was unearthed by officers. Some time before the discovery of the Bender's secret the body of a man had been found deliberately concealed under the ice of a frozen creek. The skull had been smashed and the throat so severely cut that the head was almost detached. A hole had been cut in the ice and the body pushed through it. Tracks in the snow of the river bank showed that the murderer's cart had a severely skewed wheel; one of the ruts had a decidedly zig-zag appearance. When tested the Bender's farm cart left the same tracks. It would seem that during the winter the ground in the Bender's orchard was too frozen to dig.

Officially the Bender's were never found. The search continued sporadically for the next fifty years, with many pairs of unhappy travelling ladies identified as Ma and Kate Bender.

However it seems possible that the Benders did meet justice. In his book *Celebrated Criminal Cases of America* (1910), Thomas Duke prints two letters from local police chiefs in response to his question: what happened to the Benders? One reports, "There was a vigilance committee organized to locate the Benders, and shortly afterwards Old Man Bender's wagon was found by the roadside riddled with bullets. You will have to guess the rest."

The other states, "A vigilance committee was formed, and some of them are still here, but they will not talk except to say that it would be useless to look for them, and they smile at reports of some of the family having been recently located."

It is possible that the vigilantes killed the Benders and kept it a secret. However it is also possible that living so close to the scene of such gruesome and heartless murder, the locals had to create a happy ending.

The Kidnapping of Charley Ross

The word kidnap, meaning to "nap" (or nab) a child, came into use in the late seventeenth century, when homeless children were nabbed and sold to the plantations in North America. But the first case of kidnapping, in our modern sense of the word (to seize someone for ransom) occurred in Philadelphia in 1874.

Charley and Walter Ross, four and six years old respectively, disappeared from their suburban Philadelphia home on 1 July, 1874. Walter was soon home again, recovered by a Mr Henry Peacock who had found him crying loudly in front of a downtown sweet shop. Walter's story was, for the period, a strange one. For the past four days two men had been driving past the front lawn of the Ross's stone mansion and offering the children sweets. On the fourth day Walter had suggested that they go into Philadelphia to buy some fireworks for the approaching Independence Day celebrations. The two men readily agreed, and took the children to "Aunt Susie's", a sweet shop on the corner of Palmer and Richmond street. Walter was given twenty-five cents to spend and gleefully ran into the shop. When he came out the carriage had gone.

The idea that Charley had been kidnapped did not at the time seem plausible. In fact the crime was not really established as existing; Pennsylvania had no specific law against it. The other reason why extortion seemed unlikely was that despite owning a large stone house, Christian Ross, the boy's father was only moderately wealthy. He had made his money in selling groceries but had recently gone bankrupt. At the time of the abduction he was only just beginning to break even again.

Then, on 3 July, a note from the kidnappers arrived. It was hand-written and only semi-literate. Despite the uneducated appearance of the spelling and grammar, the style was florid: ". . . if any aproch is made to his hidin place that is the signil for his instant anihilation. if you regard his lif puts no one to search for him yu money can fetch him out alive an no other existin powers . . ." The note demanded money without stating an amount, or specifying a method of payment. It was obvious that the kidnappers wished to bargain.

Ross gave the letter to the police and they made the contents public. The community was outraged in a way that perhaps is no longer imaginable. When the police decided to closely search the whole local area, the inhabitants voluntarily allowed officers to search their homes, something that the police would have had legal difficulty in compelling them to do. Anyone who refused the police entry was looked upon with suspicion. Although the child was not found, a great deal of stolen property was, and prosecutions followed.

Three days after the last another note arrived, demanding $20,000 and threatening to kill the child if any detectives were set on their trail. Ross was directed to enter a personal ad in *The Philadelphia Ledger* when he was ready to negotiate. It was decided that the longer an exchange of notes could be maintained the better the chance of forcing the kidnappers into a blunder. Therefore the ad read: "Ross will come to terms to the best of his ability."

A reply soon arrived, saying that the abductors were getting very impatient, and that the reason for the evasive reply was obvious to them. Despite this Ross continued to publish ambiguous answers. In fact, he had made up his mind not to compound a felony by paying the criminals, and went as far as to announce the fact publicly. This in effect severed the link of communication with the kidnappers and put Charley Ross' life in a great deal of danger.

Seeing that the worry of this situation was driving his wife into an early grave, Ross relented. Through the small ads he signalled his willingness to hand over the money. Shortly another note arrived, remonstrating with Ross for behaving so recklessly and postponing any deal. The reason given was that the phase of the moon was not propitious for business transactions.

On 30 July the instructions arrived at last. Ross was to put the money in a white painted suitcase and board the night train to New York with it. For the entire journey he was to stand on the rear platform of the last carriage, looking back down the track. He was to throw the suitcase off the train at the signal of a torch. It was clear that the kidnappers had been waiting for a moonless night, in order to avoid being followed.

Ross complied, and waited for the whole journey without receiving a signal. On his return a note awaited him, chiding him for failing to keep the deal. It seemed that the kidnappers had read a newspaper report "revealing" that Ross intended to go with the police to follow up a clue somewhere entirely different. Consequently they themselves had not taken the trouble to turn up. Even if the kidnappers had got hold of the case, they would have found that it contained only a letter demanding a simultaneous exchange of money for child. Ross now communicated this demand to the kidnappers. They replied that simultaneous transfer was impossible, and again threatened to kill the child.

Meanwhile the New York police had found an informer capable of identifying the handwriting of the ransom notes. According to this man the writing belonged to a William Mosher. The informant said that a few years previously Mosher and a man named Joseph Douglas had approached him to be an accomplice in abduction of a millionaire's child. The information seemed promising, and the police traced Mosher to 235 Monroe Street, Philadelphia where he lived with his family. Douglas lived in the same house. Unfortunately, by the time police searched the building the Moshers and Douglas had moved to New York.

At about the same time a final communication reached Ross. It instructed him to place an ad in *The New York Herald* reading "Saul of Tarsus: Fifth Avenue Hotel" followed by the date that he would be there with the money. Ross did as he was told, sat in the hotel all of 15 November, but there was no visitation. The kidnappers remained silent.

On 14 December the summer home of a Mr Van Brunt situated on the Upper East Side of New York was burgled. Mr Van Brunt was in residence, and heard the intruders climbing down into his cellar over the sounds of a storm. By the time that the burglars re-emerged from the cellar, there were five armed men waiting for them. Mr Van Brunt shouted "Halt!" The burglars fired two shots, both of which missed, and tried to escape out of the window. Van Brunt shot the nearest man with his shotgun, nearly blowing him in half, while his son jumped on the other burglar and accidentally shot him through the chest with a handgun. It was clear that both men were dying. Although in terrible pain, the burglar with the chest wound refused to be moved, and asked for an umbrella to keep himself dry during his last moments. In between fits of pain the man spoke: "Men, I won't lie to you. My name is Joseph Douglas and the man over there is William Mosher. He lives in New York, and I have no home. I am a single man and have no relatives except for a brother and a sister whom I have not seen for twenty years. Mosher is married and has four children" (here pain for a moment overcame his speech) "I have forty dollars in my pocket that I made honestly. Bury me with that." After another fit he continued: "Men, I am dying now and it's no use lying. Mosher and I stole Charley Ross." Van Brunt asked him why they had done it. "To make money." was the simple reply. When asked where the boy was Douglas told them to ask Mosher. He was told that Mosher was already dead, and his blasted body was dragged over in order to prove it. Douglas said that they had known that the police had them cornered. All he would say about Charley was that: "the child will be returned home safe and sound in a few days." Douglas survived over an hour of agony in the rain. Eventually he lapsed into unconsciousness and died.

The bodies were taken to the morgue, where a terrified Walter Ross identified them as the men who had taken Charley. Despite Douglas' dying assurances, and a reward of $5,000 and no questions asked for anyone who returned the child, Charley was never seen again.

Mr Ross carried on searching for his child, heartened by a statement made by William Westervelt, Mosher's brother-in-law and the man with whom Mosher and Douglas had lived in New York. He had told Ross that the day before he died, Mosher had said that he would arrange a simultaneous transfer if that was the only way to get the money. This pre-supposes that the boy was still alive.

Westervelt was tried as an accomplice in New York, and despite a lack of any firm evidence he was sentenced to seven years in solitary confinement.

It has to be assumed, despite Westervelt's statement, that Charley Ross was dead long before Mosher and Douglas were shot. Perhaps he was killed when Christian Ross announced publicly that he had no intention of aiding a felon. An unconfirmed story reports that Charley Ross was delivered into Westervelt's hands almost immediately after his kidnap, Mosher and Douglas remaining in Philadelphia to arrange ransom notes and payment. Westervelt, according to the story, became nervous and drowned the child in the East River. This was impossible to confirm however, as Westervelt disappeared after serving his sentence.

Christian Ross spent the rest of his life and his money checking up reports of Charley, travelling as far afield as Europe.

On 25 February, 1875 Pennsylvania Legislature officially recognized kidnapping as a crime.

chapter four

POISONINGS AND RAILWAY MURDERS

*O*n 25 July, 1814, *a strange contraption with iron wheels groaned and hissed into life, and dragged eight wagonloads of coal along parallel iron tracks. That first railway engine, christened "Blücher" and affectionately known as Puffing Billy, also dragged its inventor into the limelight of world history.*

George Stephenson, the self-educated son of a Northumbrian miner, was not only an inventive genius; he also proved himself an inspired prophet when he told the British House of Commons: "People will live to see the time when railroads will become the great highways for the King and all his subjects . . ." What he did not foresee was that his great invention was inaugurating a new and fascinating chapter in the history of murder.

Oddly enough, the classic cases of "murder on the railway" – Müller, Dickman, the Merstham tunnel mystery, the Rock Island express murder – now have a nostalgic fascination for students of crime. We can anticipate the day when railway stations will disappear and give way to airports – as they have already disappeared in many parts of America – and the thought of a steam engine chugging between green fields has all the charm of a pleasant daydream.

The First Railway Murder

England's first train murderer was a twenty-five-year-old German tailor named Franz Muller; indeed, he may be the world's first train murderer, for his crime was committed in 1864, and it was almost another ten years before Jesse James committed the world's first train robbery and brought a new kind of risk into the lives of railway passengers.

On the night of 9 July, 1864, at Hackney railway station, two men entered a first class compartment of a train that had come from Fenchurch Street, and noticed a bloodstained black beaver hat lying on the seat; under the seat they found a heavy walking stick with bloodstains on it. Obviously, some crime had taken place.

Soon after this, the engineer of another train noticed a bundle lying beside the line. It proved to be an old gentleman with a fractured skull. He died twenty-four hours later. Letters in his pocket identified him as Thomas Briggs, the seventy-year-old chief clerk of Robart's Bank, in the City.

The only clue was the hat made of beaver fur, which was too old and worn to belong to Mr Briggs. It seemed that the murderer had snatched up Mr Briggs's hat by accident, and left his own behind. Mr Briggs's colleagues at the bank were able to tell the police that he wore gold-rimmed glasses and carried a gold watch and chain. These were missing. His hat, apparently, was also quite distinctive, having been specially made for him; its lining was unique and easily recognizable. A few days later, a Cheapside jeweller named John Death told the police about a young foreigner who had come into his shop, and exchanged a gold watch chain for a less expensive one and a cheap ring. The watch chain was identified as belonging to the dead man.

But who was the young foreigner? Newspaper publicity about the bloodstained hat solved this problem too; a cabman named Matthews identified the beaver hat as belonging to a German called Franz Muller, who had courted his daughter for a time. Matthews had, in fact, bought the beaver hat for Muller.

UNDER THE PATRONAGE

Of the NOBILITY.

INSTANTANEOUS COMMUNICATION,

Between PADDINGTON and SLOUGH, a distance of nearly
Twenty Miles, by means of The

ELECTRIC
TELEGRAPH

Which may be seen in operation Daily, from Nine in the Morning
till Eight in the Evening, at The

GREAT WESTERN RAILWAY,

Paddington Station—and The

TELEGRAPH COTTAGE,

Close to the Slough Station.

Admission. — ONE SHILLING,
Children and Schools Half-Price.

Since this very interesting Exhibition has been opened to the Public, it has been honoured by the visits of His Royal Highness Prince Albert, the Emperor of Russia, the King, and Prince William of Prussia, the Duke de Montpensier, His Royal Highness the Duke of Cambridge, the Duke of Wellington, Sir Robert Peel, the Foreign Ambassadors, and most of the Nobility, &c.

In no way has the Science of Electricity been made so subservient to the uses of man, as in its application to the purposes of Telegraphic Communication, which is now brought to the height of perfection. The working of this beautiful Apparatus is not in the least degree affected by the weather, intelligence can be sent by night equally well as by day; distance is no object; by its extraordinary agency communications can be transmitted, to a distance of a Thousand Miles, in the same space of time, and with the same ease and unerring certainty, as a signal can be sent from London to Slough. According to the best authorities, the Electric Fluid travels at the rate of

280,000 Miles in a Second.

The Electric Telegraph has been adopted by Her Majesty's Government, and the Patentees have just completed a line of communication between London and Portsmouth, agreeably to directions received a short time ago, from

The Right Hon. the Lords of the Admiralty.

In the late trial of John Tawell, at Aylesbury, for the Murder at Salt Hill, near Slough, the Electric Telegraph is frequently mentioned in the evidence, and referred to by Mr. Baron Parke in his summing up. The Times Newspaper very justly observes, "That had it not been for the efficient aid of the Electric Telegraph, both at the Paddington and Slough Stations, the greatest difficulty, as well as delay, would have been occasioned in the apprehension of the prisoner." Although the train in which Tawell came to town was within a very short distance of the Paddington Station, before any intelligence was given at the Slough Telegraph Office, nevertheless before the train had actually arrived, not only had a full description of his person and dress been received, but the particular carriage and compartment in which he rode were accurately described, and an officer was in readiness to watch his movements. His subsequent apprehension is so well known, that any further reference to the subject is unnecessary.

The Telegraph Office, at Paddington Station, is at the End of the Up-Train Platform, where a variety of interesting apparatus may be seen in constant operation.

T. HOME, Licensee.

S. G. Fairbrother, Printer, 31, Bow Street, Covent Garden.

The police rushed to Muller's lodgings, only to find that he had already left. His landlady said he had sailed for Canada, and was now on his way to New York. Fortunately, the *Victoria* was a fairly slow boat; two detectives pursued him on the much faster *City of Manchester*, together with the jeweller and the cabman. So as Muller disembarked from the *Victoria*, he was identified by Mr Death, and the detectives arrested him.

At his trial – paid for by the German Legal Protection Society – the prosecution pointed out that Mr Briggs's watch had been found sewn in a piece of canvas in Muller's trunk. This fact made a not-guilty defense virtually impossible, and the jury lost no time in bringing in a guilty verdict. Muller protested his innocence until he stood on the gallows; then, a moment before the trap dropped, he said in German: "I have done it." As the body swung on the end of the rope, the clergyman who had administered the last rites shouted: "Confessed! Confessed!"

Muller must have been one of the most incompetent murderers of all time. The crime was committed for money, yet he only took thirty shillings and the gold watch; he left four guineas and a valuable snuffbox in his victim's pocket. By exchanging the watch chain and taking the wrong hat, he ensured his own conviction. Yet his ultimate piece of stupidity was to keep Briggs's hat, with its distinctive lining – he was actually wearing it when he was arrested.

John Tawell – Murder by a Quaker

The message that alerted train drivers to look out for Mr Briggs's body was sent by telegraph. Nineteen years earlier, one of the

The most sensational of all train murderers was the Hungarian train wrecker Sylvestre Matushka, who blew up trains because it caused him erotic excitement. Jailed for life in 1932 for causing two train wrecks in which twenty-two people were killed and over one hundred injured, he was released during World War II. He went on to work for the Americans as an explosives expert during the Korean war.

first telegraphs led to the arrest of a particularly ruthless killer. He became known as "Quaker Tawell."

John Tawell, who began life as a druggist, was transported to Australia for forgery in 1814, but by the time he returned to England, had amassed a fortune of £30,000. His wife fell ill and died, and during her illness, Tawell began a liaison with the attractive girl who nursed her, Sarah Hadler. She later bore him two children, and Tawell moved her to a cottage at Salthill, near Slough. Meanwhile, he married a second time, a Miss Catforth, from whom he took care to conceal the liaison. He paid Sarah Hadler (now known as Hart) £1 a week. After Tawell paid Sarah a visit in September 1844, she fell ill and vomited, but recovered from the attack.

On New Year's Day, 1845, Tawell went down to Salthill from his home in Berkhamsted; a neighbour saw him arrive, and a little later, met Sarah on her way to buy stout, and remarked how happy she looked. Soon after dusk, the neighbour heard Sarah scream, and went to her door with a lighted candle; she met Tawell, hurrying away, and found Sarah writhing on the floor in agony. Before the arrival of the doctor, she was dead.

A telegraph line – one of the first – had recently been constructed from Slough to Paddington, and a message was sent, asking the police to look out for a man in Quaker dress. When Tawell arrived at Paddington, he was followed to the lodging he had taken for the night, and arrested the next morning. He immediately made his first mistake by denying that he had left London the previous day.

Meanwhile, Sarah Hadler's body had been opened, and the bitter smell of prussic acid had been noted. The analyst, Mr Cooper, mixed the stomach contents with potassium ferrosulphate, and obtained the deep Prussian blue colour of potassium ferrocyanide. His conclusion was that Sarah Hadler had been poisoned by prussic acid, probably administered in stout. When it was proved that Tawell had bought the acid at a chemist shop in Bishopsgate, the case against him looked black.

The defending, counsel, Fitzroy Kelly, advanced an ingenious defence, saying that apple pips contain prussic acid, and that there had been a barrel of apples in the room in which Sarah Hadler had died. At this, both sets of medical experts proceeded to distil apple pips to see how much cyanide they could obtain.

The prosecution said that the amount distilled from 15 apples was not even dangerous; the defence replied that they had succeeded in distilling two-thirds of a grain of pure hydrocyanic acid from 15 apples, and that such a dose could be toxic.

The jury took the view that all this was irrelevant, and sentenced Tawell to death. Shortly before his execution, he confessed to the murder, and to an attempt to poison Sarah Hadler with morphine the previous September. His motive had been financial – his Australian investments had dropped in value, and he wanted to save the £1 a week he paid his mistress. Tawell was hanged in April 1845, and is now remembered mainly as the first murderer to be trapped by the electric telegraph. The defence lawyer became known forever afterwards as "Apple Pip Kelly".

Dr Palmer of Rugeley

If Muller and Tawell were both incompetents, Dr William Palmer – who became infamous as "Palmer the Poisoner" – was, on the contrary, one of the most successful criminals of the century of gaslight. During his nine-year career of crime, Palmer committed at least a dozen murders, and would probably have committed a dozen more if he had not been arrested. This came about in 1855, when he was accused of poisoning a friend named Cook with strychnine.

On 13 November 1855, Palmer and John Parsons Cook attended the races at Shrewsbury, and Cook's mare, Polestar, won. Back in a hotel in Rugeley, where they were celebrating, Cook took a swallow of his brandy and jumped to his feet crying: "Good God, there's something in that that burns my throat." Palmer retorted "Nonsense", and drained the rest of the brandy. But Cook became increasingly ill. And after taking some pills offered to him by Palmer, his body convulsed so violently that his head touched his heels, and he died a few minutes later. Palmer was not slow to claim that the dead man had negotiated £4,000 for his benefit, and produced a document to prove it.

ILLUSTRATED AND UNABRIDGED EDITION

OF

The 🦁 Times

REPORT

OF THE

TRIAL OF WILLIAM PALMER,

FOR POISONING JOHN PARSONS COOK,

AT RUGELEY.

THE TALBOT ARMS, RUGELEY, THE SCENE OF COOK'S DEATH.

FROM THE SHORT-HAND NOTES TAKEN IN THE CENTRAL CRIMINAL COURT
FROM DAY TO DAY.

LONDON: WARD AND LOCK, 158, FLEET STREET.
1856.

It was some days before Cook's stepfather became suspicious and demanded an autopsy. Palmer was arrested on a money-lender's writ. Yet, incredibly, he was not only permitted to be present at the autopsy, but to sneak out of the room with the jar containing Cook's stomach – he was caught only just in time.

Now it was recalled that Palmer had been associated with a long series of sudden deaths, and with many dubious financial transactions. As a trainee doctor he had fathered no fewer than fourteen illegitimate children, and one of these had died unexpectedly after a visit to Palmer. An acquaintance named Abbey had died in the Staffordshire Infirmary after drinking a glass of brandy with Palmer.

Back in Rugeley with his medical diploma, Palmer had married an heiress, the illegitimate daughter of an Indian army officer; but apparently she was not as rich as he had hoped. Three years later, he invited his mother-in-law to stay with them, and she died suddenly during the visit. Her money passed to her daughter – and in turn to Palmer. In the following year, a bookmaker named Bladon died with equal suddenness when staying with Palmer. A large sum of money disappeared, and so did Bladon's betting book, in which Palmer figured as a heavy loser. His wife was heard to enquire wearily: "Where will it end?" – her own sudden death would occur three years later. But in the meantime, sudden deaths continued to occur with suspicious frequency – a creditor named Bly, an uncle named "Beau" Bentley, and four of Palmer's children, who died in convulsions. Then, in 1853, Palmer insured his wife for £13,000, and she died soon afterwards. The ease with which he had acquired this money – and staved off bankruptcy – evidently decided Palmer to insure the life of his brother Walter for £82,000. But when Walter died suddenly, after a drinking bout, the company was suspicious, and refused to pay. Palmer succeeded in insuring a friend called George Bates for £25,000, who also died unexpectedly; but when a detective employed by the company learned from a boot boy that he had seen Palmer pouring something into Bates's drink, they once again refused to pay. Palmer then had a drinking session with the boot boy, who was severely ill after it.

It was after these setbacks that Palmer attended the Shrewsbury races with Cook, who died in agony a week later.

The bodies of Palmer's wife and brother were now exhumed;

and a considerable quantity of antimony was found in Anne Palmer. There was no poison in Walter Palmer, but Taylor pointed out that prussic acid would escape from the body after death in the form of gases.

Cook's stomach had been sent to the well-known Professor of Medical Jurisprudence, John Swain Taylor, at Guy's Hospital. It had been turned inside out before it had been thrown in the jar, and Palmer had then succeeded in taking the jar out of the room before anyone noticed; when it was returned, there were two slits in its parchment cap. Taylor was able to find a small quantity of antimony in the stomach – not enough to kill a man – but no strychnine. Palmer was still at large when Taylor's letter, containing his results, arrived in Rugeley, and he succeeded in intercepting the letter, and sending the coroner a present of game, pointing out that no strychnine had been found.

If the case had depended solely on Taylor's evidence, there can be no doubt that Palmer would have been acquitted. But the circumstantial evidence was overwhelming. It was proved that he had forged Cook's signature on a cheque for £350 while his friend lay ill, and also forged the document showing that Cook owed him £4,000. So although Taylor's evidence came in for some derision, there was never any doubt about the verdict, and Palmer's guilt. He was hanged at Stafford on 14 June 1856.

Dr Pritchard

Palmer is a strange phenomenon because, although born into a wealthy middle class family, he seems to have been a born crook. The same is true of that other famous Victorian poisoner, Dr Edward William Pritchard – although in his case, dishonesty seems to have been compounded with mental instability.

Pritchard was born in 1825, son of a captain in the Royal Navy. When he was twenty-one he was commissioned as an assistant surgeon in the Royal Navy, and served until he was twenty-six. At Portsmouth he met a pretty Scottish girl, whom he married. She was Mary Jane Taylor, and the husband and wife moved to Hunmanby, near Filey in Yorkshire. They had five children. Pritchard soon became known as a habitual liar and boaster in Hunmanby, and his frequent amours did much to ruin his reputation as a responsible medical man. He was a freemason, and used his membership of that body for self-advertisement. In 1858 Hunmanby became too hot to hold him and he sold his practice. For a year he travelled abroad as a medical attendant to a gentleman, and then started to practise in Glasgow. Here he soon made himself as unpopular as he had been in Yorkshire. His vanity seems to have been overwhelming, like his mendacity. He would lecture on his travels, and distribute photographs of himself to anyone who showed any tendency to admiration. He even gave one to a stranger he encountered on a train. He claimed to be a friend of Garibaldi (who had never heard of him), and when he applied for the Andersonian chair of Surgery, he submitted as testimonials the names of many eminent English doctors, who had certainly never heard of him. (He did not get the appointment.) He manufactured evidence for his friendship with Garibaldi by presenting himself with a walking-stick engraved, "from his friend General Garibaldi".

On 5 May 1863 his failing professional reputation was further damaged when a servant girl mysteriously died in a fire at his home at II Berkely Terrace, Glasgow. A verdict of death by misadventure was returned; but the girl had made no attempt to leave her bed, so it seems probable that she was unconscious when the fire started; moreover, Mrs Pritchard was absent from home that night.

Pritchard pressed a claim against a suspicious insurance company and won it.

In 1864 Pritchard moved to Sauchiehall Street, where he bought a house with money supplied by his wife's mother, Mrs Taylor. There, in the same year, his wife caught him kissing a fifteen-year-old servant-girl, Mary M'Cleod, whom he had seduced. (She became pregnant, but allowed Pritchard to perform an abortion.)

In November 1864 Mrs Pritchard fell ill, and went to stay with her family in Edinburgh, where she got better. On returning to Glasgow, she became ill again and took to her bed, where she stayed until her death in March 1865. On 8 December Pritchard bought an ounce of Fleming's Tincture of Aconite, and made three similar purchases during the next three months. A Dr Gairdner was summoned, and was so suspicious of her symptoms that he suggested to Mrs Taylor's son (also a doctor) that Mrs Pritchard should be removed from the house. Pritchard claimed that she was too ill to move, so Mrs Taylor, who was a healthy and powerful woman, although seventy years old, moved in to nurse her daughter. On the day of her arrival, she ate some tapioca (which was later found to contain antimony) and promptly fell ill. She finally died during the night of 24 February. A Dr Patterson who called suspected that she was under the influence of some powerful narcotic, and refused to give a death certificate, which Pritchard finally supplied himself, stating cause of death as apoplexy. On the week of 13 March Pritchard decided to finish poisoning his wife, which he did to such good effect that she finally died on the night of 17 March. But a cook and housemaid who had tasted some of the food eaten by Mrs Pritchard became ill, and there was considerable suspicion of the doctor. He certified the cause of death as gastric fever, and took the body to Edinburgh to be buried. On his return he was arrested on suspicion of murder. Someone had written an anonymous letter to the police (probably Dr Patterson, although he denied it). The bodies of Mrs Taylor and Mrs Pritchard were examined and both found to contain antimony and aconite. (Pritchard had declared that Mrs Taylor's death may have been caused by an overdose of a medicine containing opium.)

The trial opened at the High Court of Justiciary, Edinburgh, in July 1865, before the Lord Justice Clerk (Right Honourable John Inglis). Prosecuting were Lord Ardmillan and Lord Jerviswoode, the Solicitor-General Mr Gifford, and Mr Crichton. Defending were Mr Rutherford Clerk, Mr Watson, and Mr Brand. It was noted that the organs of both victims were impregnated with antimony, although there was no trace of it in the stomachs, pointing to poisoning over a period. During the trial, Dr Patterson showed himself extremely hostile to the prisoner. The defence tried to blame Mary M'Cleod for the poisoning, a suggestion which the judge dismissed in his summing-up. The jury found Pritchard guilty after an hour's deliberation. In prison he applied himself to his devotions, and confessed to the murders, attempting, in one confession, to implicate Mary M'Cleod, although he later admitted that he alone was responsible for the murders.

The motive of the murders is obscure, although Pritchard must surely have been a man who felt the ground slipping away from underneath him as his lies and attempts to gain admirers brought only dislike and pity, and might have decided that he needed to make a completely fresh start. He was certainly slightly insane, and his hypocrisy sometimes savours of total self-delusion; for example, when his wife's death was announced, he cried: "Come back, my dear Mary Jane. Don't leave your dear Edward." When the coffin was about to be taken to the station, Pritchard kissed his wife's lips repeatedly, muttering words of love.

His execution in Jail Square, near Hutcheson Bridge, was attended by a record crowd of 100,000.

chapter five

INFAMOUS AUSTRALIAN CASES

*A*ustralia's early record of crime, like that of America, consists mainly of acts of highway robbery and burglary. A list of the 165 criminals executed in the Melbourne jail between 1842 (the year it was opened) and 1900 includes many cases labelled "robbery with violence", "robbery with wounding", "shooting with intent to kill", "attemped murder", and in one case, "ambush of the McIvor gold escort". (The year 1880 naturally includes the execution of legendary outlaw Ned Kelly.) Rape was then a capital offense, and there are half a dozen cases of rape and carnal knowledge, including rape of a girl of ten, of a girl under six, and one entry that states simply: "Carnally knowing daughter." The severity of sentences for wounding and attempted murder is an indication that, even in 1850, this was a "frontier society" in which crime was treated with the utmost severity.

The Man They Couldn't Hang

Many of the early settlers were convicts who had been "transported" to the Botany Bay penal colony. A widely publicized case of 1803 involved a Jewish Cockney convict named Joseph Samuels, who had been transported for seven years for housebreaking in 1801, at the age of nineteen.

One night in August 1803, a local prostitute named Mary Breeze returned from a hard evening's work to find that her cottage had been ransacked; among other items missing was a portable desk with twenty-four guineas hidden in it. Mary Breeze alerted the local constable, Joseph Luker, who set off in search of the robbers. It seems that he did not get far. The next morning, his body was found on the trail near Mary Breeze's cottage. He had been killed by sixteen savage blows to the head with a cutlass.

The newspaper accounts merely state that "various clues" led the police to the cottage of a member of the "convict constabularly" – presumably an ex-convict who had now become a policeman – named Isaac Simmonds. They found Simmonds with Joseph Samuels, and two other men named William Bladders and Richard Jackson. All four were charged on "suspicion of robbery and murder". The following day in court, Samuels admitted burgling Mary Breeze's cottage, but denied the murder of Constable Luker.

Bloodstains on their clothes led to Simmonds and Bladders being charged with murder. But at their trial, they "explained away" the stains (probably alleging that they were animal blood), and were found not guilty. Twenty-one-year-old Samuels was the only one to be found guilty – of housebreaking. And since most crimes in 1803 were capital, he was sentenced to death.

At 9 a.m. on 26 September, 1803, Samuels was led out to be hanged. Simmonds was in the crowd. And when the chaplain asked him to confess his crimes before his execution, Samuels pointed at Simmonds and shouted that *he* had committed the murder, and that he and Simmonds (a fellow Jew) had taken a Hebrew oath of secrecy on the night of their arrest. (They had been kept in a cell together.)

It was too late to charge Simmonds, so the preparations for the execution went ahead. The horse pulling the cart on which Samuels was standing was urged forward. For a moment, Samuels dangled in the air. Then the rope snapped and he fell to the ground. The hangman was summoned again; he placed a second noose around Samuel's neck, and again the horse walked forward. This time, the rope somehow unravelled, and Samuels again landed on the ground. At the third attempt, Samuels was held by two men as the cart moved away, then dropped. The rope snapped again.

The Provost Marshall stopped the proceedings, and reported the strange events to the governor, who ordered a reprieve. Samuels went back to the penal settlement to a lengthened term of imprisonment. A few years later, he drowned near the Newcastle penal settlement when he and a number of other convicts stole a boat which sank in a storm.

The Kinder Case

The classic Australian murder of the age of gaslight is a typical eternal triangle – although in this case, it might be better compared to a square. It has another remarkable feature – the murderer, Louis Bertrand, was cast in the mould of the true Victorian villain – in a work of fiction he would be regarded as quite unbelievable.

Henry Kinder was a bank clerk who also happened to be an alcoholic. He and his attractive wife Ellen had moved from New Zealand to Sydney at about the same time that a dental assistant named Henri Louis Bertrand had arrived from

England's case of "the man they couldn't hang" occurred in 1885. John Lee of Babbacombe, Devon, had been sentenced to hang for the murder of his employer, Miss Emma Keyse, who had been found dead on 15 November 1884 with her throat cut. Lee was sentenced on circumstantial evidence. On 22 February, 1885, Lee was taken to the scaffold, and the hangman pulled the lever. The trapdoor – which had been repeatedly tested – refused to open. Lee was removed and the trapdoor tested; it worked perfectly. Berry the hangman tried again; again the trap jammed. There were more successful tests, then Berry tried again. When the trap refused to open a third time, Lee was taken back to his cell. His sentence was commuted to twenty-two years, and he was released on 17 December 1907. He always insisted that he had dreamed that the trap would not work the night before it happened. There was one major difference between this and the Samuels case: Lee was almost certainly guilty.

England. Bertrand even looked like a stage villain – he had dark wavy hair, parted down the middle, and a little moustache; if his pictures are to be believed, he also had dark smouldering eyes. In Sydney, the Frenchman married a girl named Jane Palmer. Apparently he treated her badly, and sometimes beat her. Nevertheless, his dental business prospered, and the two of them lived in fashionable Wynyard Square.

Unlike the gentle Jane Bertrand, Ellen Kinder required more than one man. In New Zealand she had had a lover named Frank Jackson. And when, in January 1865, she met the good looking Frenchman, she lost no time in allowing him to join her in bed. Bertrand does not seem to have concealed the affair from his wife – in fact, he even forced her to get into bed with himself and his mistress. It was later suggested that he possessed some hypnotic power over her. What is certain is that he dominated her completely.

Six months after the two became lovers, Ellen Kinder's previous lover, Frank Jackson, arrived in Sydney and went to stay with the Kinders. When Henry was at the bank, Jackson and Ellen Kinder retired to her bed.

When Bertrand found out that his mistress was being doubly unfaithful, he was indignant. There was a showdown, which ended with Bertrand demanding that she choose between them. With downcast eyes, Ellen admitted that she preferred the dentist. Jackson accepted this philosophically, and moved out.

The cunning Bertrand now saw that Frank Jackson might be of use to him. If Jackson would seduce Jane Bertrand, he would have an excuse for casting her off. Accordingly, he invited Frank Jackson to move in with them. But apparently the seduction failed to occur – either because Jackson was not attracted to Jane, or because Jane was shy and unsuited to infidelity. Bertrand shook his head. "It's a pity my wife is virtuous. It makes it so hard to get rid of her."

In fact, the devious Frenchman's plans were even more sinister. He had found a bundle of love letters from Ellen in Jackson's belongings, and was tormented with jealousy. Now he decided to kill Ellen's husband, and to implicate Jackson. After all, if Kinder was murdered, and the letters were found by the police, Jackson would be the obvious suspect . . .

Incredibly, the villainous dentist took his young assistant, Alfred Burne, into his confidence. One evening, Alfred rowed

him across the harbour, and Bertrand vanished in the direction
of the Kinder's cottage in St Leonards, clutching a tomahawk.
He returned looking disgruntled. The intended victim had been
drunk – probably in bed – and Bertrand's nerve had failed him.
A week later Alfred rowed him to the north shore again; for
some obscure reason, the dentist had blacked his face and
donned a red shirt. He asked Alfred to come along and help
him with the murder. His assistant declined, and Bertrand
cursed and ordered him to row back.

Now Bertrand bought a brace of pistols, and began practising
by firing at a sheep's head. He also warned Frank Jackson that he
intended to kill Henry Kinder, and gave him the money to go to
Melbourne. His intention was to make it look as if Jackson had
fled. In fact, Jackson only went as far as Maitland, a hundred
miles away.

Now, at last, Bertrand was ready. On Monday 2 October – the
Australian spring – Jane Bertrand spent the day at the Kinder's
cottage – Henry was home suffering from a hangover. Louis
Bertrand came over later. He and Henry went to a hotel for
a drink, and later the two couples sat in the parlour, Kinder
and Bertrand playing cards while the women arranged flowers.
There was a sudden loud report. The women looked round in
time to see Henry Kinder slump on to the carpet. Bertrand bent
down and replaced Kinder's pipe in his mouth. A smoking pistol
lay on the carpet. Ellen Kinder fled from the room, while Jane
knelt down and tended Henry Kinder, who was still alive.

A doctor who was called a few hours later was told that Kinder
had shot himself. (Bertrand apparently hoped he would have
bled to death by then, but Henry remained stubbornly alive.)
The dentist told the doctor that the Kinders had been quarrelling
about a man just before it happened – he was obviously still
determined to implicate Jackson. The doctor accepted his story
– after all, it was supported by both wives. He did not notice
that Kinder's wound was at an angle – behind the ear – that
made it highly unlikely that he had fired the pistol.

Henry Kinder was still able to speak, and told the police that
he had *not* shot himself; they decided that he was delirious and
ignored him. But, to Bertrand's chagrin, Kinder now began to
recover. Jane Bertrand was nursing him faithfully. So Bertrand
ordered her to put poison in Kinder's milk. Whether she did
or not was never established; at all events, the following day,

Kinder was dead. It was assumed, naturally, that he had finally died from his wound.

So it seemed that the scheming dentist had committed the perfect crime. Now all he had to do was to get rid of his wife, and he could marry his mistress. But a new complication arose. Frank Jackson heard of Kinder's death, and wrote to Bertrand threatening to denounce him unless Bertrand paid him £20 to leave the country. But Bertrand felt secure in the suicide verdict. He handed the letter over to the police, who charged Jackson with blackmail; he was sentenced to twelve months.

The dentist's sister Harriet Kerr now came to stay with him. She adored her brother, and it was natural that he should tell her of his love affair with Ellen. But when she saw the way he treated his wife, she was disgusted – and even more so when Jane removed her dress and showed her whiplash marks on her back. Unaware that he was losing her admiration, Bertrand even admitted that he had killed Henry Kinder. His sister burst into tears.

One morning soon after this, Harriet returned from a walk to hear her brother shouting at his wife. He was brandishing a heavy stick, and she was whimpering: "Don't kill me – you promised you wouldn't." Harriet burst in, and was ordered out. She went as far as the landing, and heard her brother order Jane to write a note saying that she had poisoned herself. His next move, clearly, was to force poison down her throat. But Jane refused. Moments later, Bertrand stormed out of the room.

Three weeks after her husband's death, Ellen Kinder and her two children left Sydney for Bathurst, where her parents lived. She and her lover exchanged passionate letters. She was sensible enough to burn his; he kept hers, and they were later produced at his trial.

And now, in the best tradition of Victorian melodrama, the villain began to go to pieces. He declared he was being haunted by the ghost of Henry Kinder, and he once pushed aside a glass of wine, saying that it reminded him of blood. He also forgot himself so far as to attack a woman named Mary Robertson – who made some slighting remarks about Ellen Kinder – with a knife. For this he received a sentence of fourteen days in jail.

Also in prison, Frank Jackson was telling the police about the murder plot. But before their investigation had progressed beyond a few enquiries, Bertrand's sister Harriet went to the police and reported his confession. Her brother was still in jail, so there was no need to arrest him. But Ellen Kinder was arrested in Bathurst, and Jane Bertrand was also taken into custody. Both women were later discharged for lack of evidence against them.

Bertrand's trial, with its scandalous evidence about adultery – even of forcing his wife to join him in bed with Ellen Kinder – was Australia's trial of the century. Bertrand deliberately behaved in a deranged manner, striding up and down the dock. And in spite of the damning evidence of his sister, Frank Jackson and Alfred Burne, the jury was unable to agree on a verdict.

At the second trial, the evidence from the first was read aloud. This time, the jury took two hours to reach a verdict of guilty. But the attempt to save time by reading the evidence aloud was to backfire. After Bertrand had been sentenced to death, the local Jewish community, led by Bertrand's wealthy uncle, briefed a barrister to try to overturn the death sentence. The main objection was that the jury should have heard the evidence from witnesses, not at second hand from transcripts of the first trial. Bertrand's sentence was commuted to life imprisonment. At which point, he brought the melodrama to a fitting conclusion by admitting his guilt.

Twenty-eight years later, he was released from prison, and immediately boarded a steamer for England. What became of him after that is unknown.

The cause of all the trouble, Ellen Kinder, returned to New Zealand, and is said to have supported herself as a barmaid.

Frederick Bailey Deeming

If the murder of Henry Kinder was Australia's crime of the century, Frederick Bailey Deeming, hanged in Melbourne jail on 23 May, 1892, was certainly its criminal of the century. He shared with Palmer the Poisoner a delight in devious criminal schemes that is reminiscent of Conan Doyle's Professor Moriarty.

Little is known of Deeming's early life. He himself claimed that both his mother and father had been in mental homes, and that as a child his own abnormality earned him the nickname, "Mad Fred".

His career of crime seems to have started relatively late. In 1883 he was about thirty years of age, and had left his recently married wife in Birkenhead while he went to Australia to seek his fortune. In Sydney he worked as a gasfitter, and very quickly spent some time in jail for stealing fittings. This is the only crime that can be said to be unworthy of Deeming's flamboyant personality; for, like Dr Pritchard, he was a braggart and inventor of tall tales worthy of Munchausen. After a brief term in jail, he made an attempt to earn an honest living, having now been joined by his wife. This failed, owing to his total unreliability, which sent his trade to his more staid rivals. He filed a petition for bankruptcy, and was arrested for fraud. Released on bail, he fled with his wife and children to Port Adelaide. There, under the name of Ward, he stayed in January 1888. It seems that he decided quite definitely on a criminal career at this time. He left there for St Helena, and on the voyage defrauded two brothers named Howe of £60. From St Helena the family moved to Cape Town, where he obtained work from a firm of engineers. He soon tired of this, and moved around to Port Elizabeth, Kimberley, Johannesburg, and Durban, always "talking big" and managing to support himself with various minor frauds. His chief prey were jewellers, and he was soon wanted for frauds amounting to £1,000 by jewellers in Cape Town, Durban, and Johannesburg. His usual method was to pose as the manager of a diamond mine.

In Johannesburg he offered lavish hospitality to big business men and gained a large sum through a swindle worked on the National Bank.

Next he obtained a post as manager of a gold-mining company at Klerksdorp. Here he devised a new swindle; he offered to sell certain gold mines to a rich financier. When the financier set off for Cape Town to investigate Deeming's claims, his agent, a man named Grice, received a telegram instructing him to pay Deeming "not more than £2,200". Grice actually paid up £2,800 for some deeds of property. Soon, Grice received a telegram from Deeming saying he intended to meet a Mr Leevy in Cape Town; soon after that, "Leevy" himself telegraphed to say that Deeming had died after a brief illness.

Deeming now sent his wife and children (there were now

four) to England, and went to Aden on a coal vessel, then to
Southampton. Detectives were on his trail, and he went from
Hull to Birkenhead, then to Camberwell, Stockton-on-Tees,
sailed for Australia, doubled back at Port Said and returned
to England.

At Hull and Beverley in Yorkshire, he was a millionaire and
a relative of Sir Wilfred Lawson. He proposed marriage to the
landlady of his hotel, who had the sense to refuse him; another
woman, a Miss Matheson, accepted him and he married her
bigamously. A few months later he deserted her. Shortly before
the marriage he was in Antwerp posing as Lord Dunn. After
the marriage he and his "wife" stayed at Gosport at the Star
Hotel under the name of Lawson; he paid the hotel bill with
a bogus cheque and returned to Hull.

In Hull, he swindled a jeweller out of £285 worth of jewellery
(paid for with a bouncing cheque) and hastily embarked for
South America. On this trip he became well known to the
passengers as a hospitable and wealthy man, manager of a
diamond mine in South Africa; he arranged a concert in aid of
the Seamen's Orphanage and headed the subscription list with
a generous donation. His fellow passengers were startled when
he was arrested at Montevideo. He wrote indignantly to his
counsel that the prison fare was doing "considerable hingery"
to his health. (Deeming seems to have been almost illiterate.) On
the way back to England he tried all kinds of ruses for escaping;
he even told the sceptical detective hair-raising adventure stories
in which he had killed men.

At Hull Assizes, on 16 October 1890, he was sentenced to
nine months in jail. On 16 July 1891 he was released. He now
went to the Commercial Hotel, Liverpool, where he posed as
O. A. Williams, who was an inspector of regiments in South
Africa (or India – his story varied), who had come to England to
take a house for a Colonel Brooks who would be shortly retiring.
Deeming was certainly now planning to murder his wife and
family, for he found a cottage, Dinham Villa, at Rainhill, and
specified that he was to concrete the kitchen floor since the
colonel hated uneven floors. His wife came to visit him at
Rainhill and had meals with him in the hotel, where she was
introduced as his sister. (Deeming was already courting a Miss
Mather, daughter of a widow who kept a newsagent's, shop.)
Towards the end of July 1891, Mrs Deeming and the children

moved into Dinham Villa, and were murdered and buried under
the kitchen floor. Deeming then cemented the floor himself,
getting workmen to help with the finishing touches. Before
leaving the hotel, where he had made many friends, he gave
a dinner party that was reported in the local papers. This was
a month after the murders. He spent two weeks in London,
where he wrote to his murdered wife's father, saying that he
intended to visit him soon with his wife, and then returned to
Rainhill, where he married Miss Mather. He took her to see
Dinham Villa, and danced a little jig on the kitchen floor.

They decided to sail for Australia. Before leaving England,
Deeming tried one more fraud; he sent a picture by rail, and
then tried claiming that it was damaged, and demanded £50
compensation. The railway company called his bluff, and he
left England without the money.

Miss Mather appears to have been extremely happy with her
lively husband; but by the time they reached Australia – ten
days before Christmas, 1891 – she must have had her doubts. A
neighbour who saw her described her as a silent woman whose
eyes seemed red from weeping. She must have suspected her
husband's true character from the fact that he now insisted on
an alias of Droven or Drewen. They took a house in Andrew
Street, Windsor, Melbourne. In a very short time indeed, Miss
Mather found her way under the bedroom floor, where she was
cemented in.

On 5 January, Deeming moved out. He applied to a matri-
monial agency for a wife, but then left Melbourne suddenly
and sailed for Sydney. On the boat he met his next prospective
victim, a Miss Katie Rounsfell, who quickly agreed to marry him.
She knew him as Baron Swanston. He travelled to Sydney with
her, then left her and obtained a job with Fraser's gold mine,
Southern Cross. She was actually on her way to join him
when chance – in the form of the discovery of Miss Mather
– saved her.

Eight weeks after Deeming had moved out of Andrew Street,
the agent, a man named Connor, went to look over the place,
having heard of an offensive odour in the bedroom. The newly
cemented fireplace was crumbling – the heat of an Australian
summer had dried it too quickly. Connor kicked away a few
lumps of soft concrete and found himself looking at the face of
a dead girl.

"Drewen" had left many clues behind him, including a card labelled O. A. Williams, with the Rainhill address on it. This soon led to the discovery of the bodies in Dinham Villa. Detective-Sergeant Considine, of the CID in Melbourne (who was in charge of the case) has declared that three houses in which Deeming had lived in Johannesburg also revealed bodies of women under the hearths. If so, it is not known who these women were. At the time Deeming lived in Johannesburg, his wife was with him.

Considine soon discovered that "Drewen" was a confidence swindler who had defrauded a Melbourne firm of valuable jewellery, and had tried to swindle another firm of £2,000. He had also tried to blackmail the shipowners whose boat had brought him to Melbourne, declaring that his wife had lost a £1,000 necklace on the trip. (No doubt this accounted for Emily Mather's disillusion, for she must have been called upon to substantiate Deeming's story.)

Deeming was traced to Southern Cross and arrested there. He was taken to Melbourne – great crowds gathering to watch his arrival – and tried there. He suffered from fits (as he had on the voyage back from Montevideo), but detectives suspected these were faked. At one point he narrowly escaped lynching. He wrote to Miss Rounsfell, declaring his innocence and asking her to believe in him; he also asked for money. (Miss Rounsfell was an heiress.)

His defence tried an insanity plea, and Deeming declared that the apparition of his dead mother frequently appeared to him, and had once urged him to kill all his woman friends. He also made a speech declaring that Emily Mather was still alive and that the people in court were the ugliest he had ever seen in his life. He was sentenced to death. In jail he confessed to being Jack the Ripper – an impossibility since he was in jail at the time of the murders.

• chapter six •

THE SCIENCE OF DETECTION

*T*he most remarkable achievement of the Age of Gaslight was undoubtedly its development of the science of detection. Scientific crime detection had been taking slow, hesitant steps since the last quarter of the eighteenth century, when a number of brilliant chemists – Scheele, Hahnemann, Metzger, Rose – learned how to detect arsenic, even after it had been absorbed by the human body – it was this new knowledge that convicted Anna Zwanziger. By 1820, the great Mathieu Orfila had created the science of toxicology, which meant that poison was no longer the murderer's most reliable weapon.

The art of photography also came to play an important part in crime detection. By the 1870s, most police forces in Europe added a photograph of a criminal to his file. Their main problem was the popularity of beards – a photograph of one bearded, scowling face looked very much like another. Moreover, an archive of a hundred thousand photographs is useless unless they are classified in a way that enables the police to decide where to start looking.

Alphonse Bertillon.

When parts of a woman's body — including her head — were found in the river Seine in 1887, photographs of the head were sold at newsagents in an attempt to identify her. Hundreds were bought. This led to her identification as the wife of an old soldier called Billoir. His defense was that he had kicked her in the course of a drunken quarrel and that she had collapsed and died. But medical examination showed that her heart had still been beating when she was dismembered. Billoir was sentenced to death, remarking gloomily: "The doctors have done for me."

Alphonse Bertillon

When the twenty-five-year-old Alphonse Bertillon became a clerk at the Sûreté in 1879, most of the old identification procedures were practically useless. Bertillon was a dreary, pedantic young man whom most people found rather repellent; but he came from a cultured and scientific family, and the chaos irritated him. He was certain there *ought* to be some simple way of arranging the hundred thousand photographs and descriptions.

Bertillon's story would be ideal for Hollywood. He compared photographs of criminals to see if there was some way of classifying noses and faces. Then he thought it might be a good idea to take measurements of criminals when they were arrested – height, reach, circumference of head, height sitting down, length of left hand, left foot, left leg – Bertillon chose the left-hand side because it was unlikely to be affected by work. He was subject to constipation, stomach upsets, headaches and nosebleeds; but he had a certain stubbornness that made him ignore the knowing smiles of colleagues. A doctor named Adolphe Quetelet had asserted that the chances of two people being exactly the same height are four to one. If that was so, and the same thing applied to the other statistics, then you needed only two or three measurements of each criminal to raise the odds to a hundred to one. When the prefect of police ignored Bertillon's letter about this method, Bertillon bought himself a set of filing cards, and started to work on his own, staying in the office until late at night. His boss Gustave Macé revealed a lack

of insight when he read Bertillon's report, and said it was too
theoretical. The prefect, Andrieux, told Bertillon to stop making
a nuisance of himself. And three years went by before Bertillon
could persuade a new prefect, Jean Camecasse, to give him an
interview. Camecasse was as sceptical as his predecessor, but
he was impressed by the clerk's persistence. He told Bertillon
that they would introduce his method experimentally for three
months. This was obviously absurd; it would take more than
three months to build up a file, and a method like Bertillon's
depended on accumulation. But with Macé himself opposed
to the whole idea, he knew his only chance lay in working
on and praying for luck. His card index swelled at the rate
of a few hundred a month. But with more than twenty
thousand criminals in Paris alone, the chances of identifying
one of them was low. Towards the end of the third month,
Bertillon had towards two thousand cards. Theoretically, his
chance of identification was one in ten – fairly high. But it must
be remembered that a large number of his criminals were sent
to jail, often for years, so most of his file was lying fallow, so
to speak.

On 20 February 1883, luck was with him. His system led
him to identify a petty criminal who had been measured three
months earlier. It was a very small triumph, but it was enough
to make Camecasse decide to allow the experiment to continue.
This was not far-sightedness. The post of prefect was a political
appointment; Camecasse was hoping for fame. Unfortunately,
a new prefect had been appointed by the time Bertillon became
a celebrity; but history allows Camecasse the credit. As the file
swelled, identification became more frequent. Before long, it
averaged one a day. But what Bertillon needed was a really
sensational case.

He had to wait until 1892 for it, but when it came, it spread
his name all over the world. And the reason for the notoriety
of the case was more or less accidental.

Since the early 1880s, a terrifying group of people known
as the Anarchists became steadily more well known. People
were not all that interested in their idealistic doctrine of the
inherent goodness of human nature – which means that man
does not need Authority to keep him virtuous. In 1881, Russian
anarchists – they called themselves Narodniki – blew up Tsar
Alexander II with a bomb; in Chicago, in May 1884, someone

hurled a home-made bomb into a crowd of policemen who were about to break up a meeting of strikers, killing seven of them. Eight anarchists were condemned to death; one of them blew himself up with a bomb, and wrote in his own blood: "Long live Anarchy!" Four of the anarchists were eventually hanged. In France, anarchists like Malatesta, Grave and Reclus spoke darkly of the "propaganda of the deed", and the bourgeoisie shuddered. On May Day 1891, three anarchists were arrested for taking part in demonstrations at Clichy, and badly beaten-up by the police. At their trial, the prosecuting attorney Bulot demanded the death penalty for all three – although no one had been killed in the riots. The judge, Benoist, acquitted one of them and gave the other two prison sentences of three and five years. In March the following year – 1892 – a tremendous explosion shook the house in which Judge Benoist lived, destroying the stairway. Two weeks later, another explosion blew up Bulot's house in the Rue de Clichy. Luckily, no one was killed in either explosion. But the panic was tremendous. Large quantities of dynamite had been stolen from quarries at Soiry, and the Parisians wondered where the next explosion would occur. A Left-Wing professor was arrested for the first explosion, and he agreed that he had planned it; however, a man named Ravachol had carried it out. Ravachol was known to the police – not as an anarchist, but as a burglar who was suspected of murder; he had killed an old miser and his housekeeper, two women who kept a hardware store, and an old miser who lived in a forest hut. He was also believed to have robbed the tomb of a countess to steal her jewellery. The alias of this forty-year-old criminal seemed to be Konigstein.

On the day of the Rue de Clichy dynamiting, Ravachol dined in the Restaurant Véry in the Boulevard Magenta, and tried to convert a waiter named Lhérot to anarchism. Two days later, he returned, and Lhérot noticed a scar on his thumb, which had been mentioned in descriptions of Ravachol. He notified the police, and the man was arrested.

Here was Bertillon's chance to prove his system to the world. Luckily, "Konigstein" had been briefly under arrest at St Etienne as a suspect in the murder of the old man, and the police there had taken his measurements before he managed to escape. Bertillon himself measured Ravachol, and the measurements corresponded exactly. The idealistic anarchist

Ravachol was the murderous criminal Konigstein, and for the time being, at least, the anarchist movement was discredited. On the evening before Ravachol's trial, the Restaurant Véry was blown up by a bomb, which killed the proprietor and a customer – it was obviously retaliation for the arrest of Ravachol, and an attempt to intimidate the judges. It succeeded; Ravachol was only condemned to prison. But the judges of St Etienne were less scared of anarchist bombs; with Bertillon's proof in their hands, they were able to bring home the five murders to Ravachol, and he was executed on 10 July 1892. For the next few years Paris rocked with bombs – there was even one in the Chamber of Deputies – and President Carnot himself was assassinated. Bertillon luckily escaped the wrath of the anarchists.

The method of Fingerprinting

But, absurdly enough the method known as "Bertillonage", which had revolutionized almost every police force in the world, was already out of date by this time. In India in the 1860s, a civil servant named William Herschel had observed that no two fingerprints are ever alike. He put it to use in his job of paying off pensioned Indian soldiers. These men could seldom write, and they all looked alike to English eyes. And when they realized this, the pensioners began collecting their pensions twice, or returned and collected other people's pensions. When Herschel noticed that fingerprints were always different, he made them sign for their pensions by placing the index finger on an inked pad, and pressing it gently at the side of his name on the list. The swindling ceased. Some years later, a Scot named Henry Faulds made the same discovery, and wrote a letter to *Nature*, declaring that this might be a means of identifying criminals. The year was 1880, two years before Bertillon was allowed to start making his experiments in measurement. Faulds and Herschel were later to be involved in bitter disputes about priority, but these do not concern us here.

A disciple of Darwin, Sir Francis Galton, became interested in Bertillonage because he thought it would help in the study of problems of heredity. He became friendly with Bertillon, and this interest in police work led him to write to Herschel about his methods of fingerprinting; he had read the exchange of letters between Herschel and Faulds in *Nature*. Galton settled down to the study of fingerprints, and soon decided that there were only four basic classifications; the core of his method was the triangle, or "delta", in the centre of a fingerprint. In 1892, Galton's book *Fingerprints* came out. So in the year of his greatest triumph, Bertillon had become redundant. He refused to acknowledge it – for years he fought grimly for his system, betraying an unfortunate lack of the truly scientific spirit. But fingerprinting was bound to prevail in the end; it was so much simpler than Bertillonage.

The first murder ever to be solved by a fingerprint took place in Necochea, Argentina. A twenty-six-year-old woman named Francesca Rojas ran into the hut of a neighbour saying that her children had been murdered. The two children, aged four and six, lay dead in bed, their heads beaten in. She accused a man named Velasquez, who was in love with her. She wanted to marry another man, and she claimed that Velasquez had threatened to kill "what she loved most". She had returned from work to find the children dead . . .

Velasquez was arrested and badly beaten, but he denied the murders, while agreeing to the threat. The police methods in Necochea were primitive; they tortured Velasquez for a week, without result; then the police chief tried making moaning noises outside the woman's hut, hoping to frighten her into confession by pretending to be a ghost.

A police inspector named Alvarez went out to investigate from La Plata. And he knew something about the work of a Dalmatian named Juan Vucetich, head of the Statistical Bureau of Police in Buenos Aires, who had developed his own fingerprint system after reading an article by Galton. Alvarez went into the woman's hut and searched for clues. All he could find was a bloody thumb-print on a door. Alvarez sawed off the portion of the door and took it back to headquarters. Then he sent for Francesca Rojas, and made her give her thumb-print. Alvarez knew very little about classification, but it was quite obvious that the two prints were identical. When he showed

Alfred Stratton.

Albert Stratton.

the woman the two prints through a magnifying glass, she broke down and confessed – she had murdered her own two children because she wanted to marry a young lover who objected to them. This Argentine Lady Macbeth, who tried to rid herself of illegitimate children and an unwanted lover with one blow, obviously deserves to stand very high on a list of the world's worst women.

The Stratton Brothers

The first English murder case involving fingerprints took place in Deptford in 1905. At 7.15 a.m., on 27 March of that year, a passing milkman saw two men emerge from a shop at 34 High Street, Deptford, and slam the door behind them. It was a paint shop, and the manager, an elderly man called Farrow, ran the shop with his wife.

At half past eight, the shop boy arrived and found the place closed up; he went to fetch the shop's owner, and they forced a kitchen window. Farrow was found dead on the ground floor, his head battered in; his wife was found dead in bed. What had happened was clear enough. The two men had broken into the shop, and Mr Farrow had heard the noise and hurried downstairs – where he was beaten over the head with jemmies and left for dead. The men went upstairs, and killed his wife in the same way. They found the cash box under her husband's pillow and emptied it. Farrow was not dead; after the men left the shop he staggered to the door and looked outside, where he was seen by a little girl who thought nothing of a bloodstained man; then he locked the shop door, and died.

The police were on the scene by 9.30, and soon found a thumb-print inside the cash box. It was photographed and enlarged. The police now checked on local criminals, and discovered that two brothers named Stratton were missing from their usual haunts. They were known as a violent and brutal pair, who had been in the hands of the police several times. They were picked up later in the week and fingerprinted. The thumb-print in the cash box was identical with that of the elder brother, Alfred. The police had no other evidence against them, since the milkman had been unable to identify them. Sergeant Collins, the fingerprint expert, would be the most important prosecution witness.

It was obviously an important case, and the future of fingerprinting might stand or fall by it – for a few years at least. Neither the judge – an elderly gentleman named Channell – nor the jury knew anything about fingerprints. The defence decided to take no chances, and called two of their own fingerprint experts. One of these was none other than Henry Faulds, the Scot who had discovered fingerprinting and declared that it should be used for police work. Through an unfortunate accident, he had never received the credit that was his due. When Sir Francis Galton had written to ask *Nature* for the addresses of the two men who had been conducting a correspondence about fingerprinting, the editor accidentally sent him only the address of Herschel. Herschel, like Galton, was a generous and disinterested sort of person, who immediately handed Galton all his results – with the consequence that Galton never had reason to consult Faulds. But Faulds, unfortunately, was an obsessive egoist who wanted credit for his discovery. (It will be remembered that Herschel actually discovered fingerprinting first, but Faulds was the first to publish the discovery.) For years, Faulds fought a violent battle to gain recognition; the British felt this was rather unsporting, and ignored him. So now Faulds decided to make himself felt by opposing the Crown case. The other "expert" was yet another disappointed egoist, Dr Garson, who had first sneered at fingerprinting (he was a champion of Bertillonage), then decided to change horses, and invented his own system. And it was Garson's appetite for recognition that swung the case against the Strattons. Sergeant Collins gave a lecture on fingerprints and drew sketches on a blackboard. Garson and Faulds made no attempt to deny that no two fingerprints are ever alike, but they *did* assert that the print on the cash box was not identical with the print of Alfred Stratton's thumb. To the judge and jury, all fingerprints looked alike, and they were inclined to credit the assertion that the two prints were not really identical. Collins replied that the discrepancies were the kind that are bound to occur when fingerprints are taken, because lines will look thicker or thinner according to the pressure applied and the angle at which the finger is

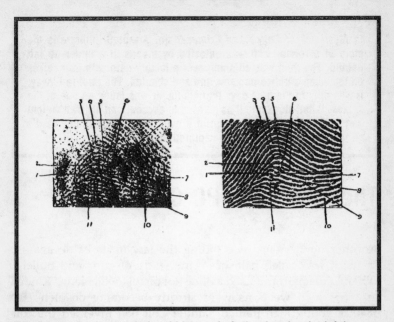

The fingerprint that made legal history. *Left*: the thumb-print left by Thomas Farrow's murderer on the cash box that he robbed. *Right*: the thumb-print of Alfred Stratton. A convincing eleven points of similarity prove beyond any doubt that they were made by the same person.

pressed on to the paper. He demonstrated this convincingly by taking fingerprints of the jury on spot, and showing exactly the same discrepancies. But the seeds of doubt had been sown. The prosecutor now played his trump card. Garson was called back to the stand, and was asked whether it was not true that he had written a letter offering to testify for the prosecution? Yet he was now testifying for the defence. Clearly, this was a man who would change his opinions for the sake of being an important witness in an important trial. The judge remarked that he was obviously untrustworthy. And the last hope of the Stratton brothers vanished. They were found guilty, and both of them proceeded to shout abuse at the court, dissipating the impression of wronged innocence they had been aiming for. The judge sentenced them to death. England's first fingerprint murder had established that a fingerprint alone is enough to hang a man.

In *Mysteries of Police and Crime*, Major Arthur Griffiths tells the story of a robber who was detected by means of a finger he left behind. The thief was climbing over a factory gate with iron spikes on top when a policeman saw him and shouted. The thief ran away; it was only in the next days that his finger was found on one of the spikes. It had stuck into it as he tried to escape, and his own weight had pulled it off. The fingerprint proved to be in Scotland Yard's collection, and the thief was captured and sentenced to jail.

The Murder of PC Cole

Another new science was aiding the law in its battle against crime; it was called ballistics – the study of guns and bullets. When Louis Bertrand used a one-shot pistol to kill Henry Kinder in 1865, such weapons were already becoming obsolete. By 1840, a young man named Samuel Colt had invented the colt revolver. By 1870, mass produced revolvers were producing a crime epidemic like the poisoning epidemic of the seventeenth century. The revolver seemed a boon for criminals, since every bullet apparently looked alike. Yet even before scientists learned to study the "rifle marks" on bullets under a microscope, the police were learning that a bullet could convict a criminal just as surely as a fingerprint. Major Arthur Griffiths cites the classic case that has become known as "Orrock's chisel."

On 1 December 1882, the cobbled, gaslit streets of east London were wrapped in choking fog as a young constable set out from Dalston police station on a beat that took him down a narrow thoroughfare called Ashwin Street. As he turned the corner, he came to a sudden halt as he saw a man placing a lantern on top of the wall outside the Baptist chapel, and beginning to scramble over. PC Cole took a swift step forward, laid his hand on the man's shoulder, and asked: "What do you think you're doing?" For a moment, the man – who seemed little more than a youth – looked as if he was going to resist; then he changed his mind and agreed to "go quietly". But PC Cole and his captive had only gone as far as the pub on the corner when the man broke loose and ran. Cole ran after him and grabbed him by the left arm; as he did so, the man reached into his pocket, pulled out a revolver, and fired three shots. A woman who was walking towards them screamed and fled; as she ran, she heard another shot. Moments later, she encountered two policeman in Dalston Lane, and led them back to the scene of the shooting. PC Cole was lying on the pavement outside the Baptist chapel, his head in the gutter; a trickle of blood ran from the bullet hole behind his left ear. He died five minutes after being admitted to the local German Hospital.

Inspector Glass, who took charge of the case, ordered a search of the area where the policeman had been found; on the wall of the Baptist chapel, the burglar had left his dark lantern; behind the railings, a chisel, a jemmy, and a wooden wedge had been left on the ground. The only other clue was a black billycock hat, which the burglar had lost in the course of the struggle. The woman who had seen him running away described him as short and slightly built; another witness gave the same description.

There was one man in the Dalston police station who believed he knew the identity of the murderer. Only minutes before Cole had arrested the burglar, Police Sergeant Cobb had been walking along Ashwin Street with another sergeant, Branwell, when they had noticed a man standing under a streetlamp. Cobb recognized him as a young cabinetmaker named Tom Orrock, and when he saw the policeman, he looked furtive and uncomfortable. Orrock had no criminal record, but he kept bad company – thugs and professional criminals – and it seemed a reasonable assumption that he would one day try his hand at crime. As they passed Orrock that night, Cobb had been tempted to arrest him for loitering. But standing under a streetlamp was no crime, and Cobb had decided against it. Now he regretted it, and was inclined to blame himself for the death of PC Cole, who was a young married man with children.

Informed of Sergeant Cobb's suspicions, Inspector Glass was inclined to be dismissive – to begin with, he disliked Cobb, regarding him as too unimaginative and too conscientious. But he ordered Tom Orrock – who was nineteen – to be brought in for an identity parade. When the witnesses who had glimpsed Cole's captive failed to identify him, Orrock was released. Soon after that, he disappeared from his usual haunts.

Months after the murder, the investigation was at a standstill. The clues seemed to lead nowhere. The hat bore no marks of identification, and the chisels and the large wooden wedge might have belonged to anybody. But the bullets looked more promising. All four had been recovered – two from the policeman's skull, one from his truncheon, another from the truncheon case. They were unusual in that they had been fired from a revolver that was little more than a toy – the kind of thing ladies sometimes carried in their handbags. The science of ballistics was unknown in 1882, but the rarity of a gun suggested that it might one day provide a valuable piece of evidence.

When studied through a magnifying glass, one of the chisels also yielded an interesting clue. A series of scratches near the handle looked like an attempt at writing, probably with a sharp nail. And when the chisel was photographed for the case file, the letters could be seen more clearly, and they resolved themselves into a capital R, followed by what looked like an o, a c, and a k. Rock. Could it be short for Orrock? Cobb began calling in every tool shop in the Hackney and Dalston area, asking if they recognized the chisels, but met with no success.

Cobb refused to give up. A year after the murder, he was talking with an acquaintance of the missing cabinetmaker named Henry Mortimer, who occasionally acted as a police informer. And Mortimer's rambling discourse suddenly arrested the sergeant's attention when he mentioned that Tom Orrock had possessed a revolver – a nickel-plated, pin-fire miniature affair. Orrock had seen it advertised in the *Exchange and Mart*, and he and Mortimer had gone to Tottenham to purchase it from the owner for the sum of half a guinea. They had also been accompanied by two men named Miles and Evans, both professional – if unsuccessful – criminals. On the way home, the four men had stopped on Tottenham Marshes and used a tree for target practice. At Cobb's request, Mortimer accompanied him to Tottenham and showed him the tree. The following day, Cobb returned alone, and dug some bullets out of the tree with his penknife. One of them was relatively undamaged, and was obviously of the same calibre as the bullets that had been fired at PC Cole.

Now Cobb was sure he had his man, and that view was confirmed when Mortimer admitted that Orrock had virtually confessed to killing PC Cole. When Mortimer had expressed disbelief, Orrock had replied: "If they can prove it against me, I'm willing to take the consequences." This is precisely what Cobb now set out to do.

The first step was to lay the new evidence before his immediate superior. Inspector Glass was still inclined to be indifferent, but he agreed to ask for help from New Scotland Yard in trying to trace the shop that had sold the chisel. And it was the Scotland Yard team that finally located a woman named Preston, a widow who carried on her husband's tool-sharpening business. She recognized the chisel because she always made a practice of scratching the name of the owner near the handle; she remembered the young man who brought in the chisel for grinding had given the name Orrock, which she had shortened to "Rock".

Now at last, they had the kind of evidence that might impress a jury. All that remained was to locate Tom Orrock. Scotland Yard was asked to circulate his description to every police station in the country. This would normally have brought prompt results, for in those days before the population explosion, most police stations were aware of any strangers who had moved into their district. So when another year failed to bring news of the wanted man, Glass was inclined to assume either that he was dead or that he had gone abroad. Cobb refused to believe it. And one day he had an inspiration. One place where a man could "lie low" with reasonable chance of escaping recognition was prison. Once again, Cobb began painstaking enquiries – enquiries that entitle him to be ranked with Canler and Macé as a distinguished practitioner of the needle-in-the-haystack method. And he soon learned that a man answering Orrock's description had been serving a term for burglary in Coldbath Fields for the past two years. Coldbath Fields, in Farringdon Road, was one of London's newer prisons, and had a reputation for severity. The name under which the prisoner was serving his sentence was not Tom Orrock, and when he was summoned to the governor's office, the man denied that he was called Orrock or had ever been in Dalston. Sergeant Cobb attended an identity parade, and had to admit reluctantly that he was unable to recognize Orrock among the seven uniformed convicts who now faced him. But as the men filed out again, they passed under a light, and Cobb suddenly recognized the profile of the man he had last seen standing under a gaslamp in Dalston more that two years earlier. He stepped forward and laid his hand on the shoulder of Thomas Henry Orrock.

Now it was a question of building up the web of circumstantial evidence. Orrock's sister, Mrs Bere, was questioned, and admitted that on the night of the murder her brother had returned home with a torn trouser leg, and without his hat, claiming that he had been involved in a street brawl. Orrock's two friends Miles and Evans were questioned separately. They admitted that they had spent the day of the murder drinking with Tom Orrock in various pubs, and that soon after 10 o'clock in the evening, the three had been in the Railway Tavern in Ashwin Street when Orrock boasted that he intended to embark on a criminal career by "cracking a crib" – stealing the silver plate of the Baptist church, which he attended regularly, and taking it to his brother-in-law to be melted down. Orrock had then left the pub. Not long after, Miles and Evans heard the sound of revolver shots, but claimed they had taken them for fog signals. All the same, they had left the pub and been among the crowd that gathered around the wounded policeman. Three weeks later, when a reward of £200 had been offered for information leading to the capture of the murderer, Orrock went to Evans and begged him not to inform on him; Evans swore that he would not "ruck" on a comrade even for a thousand pounds.

But all this was merely hearsay evidence. The vital link between Tom Orrock and the murder of PC Cole was the revolver. This had disappeared – one witness said that Orrock admitted throwing it into the River Lea. But the police were able to track down the man who had sold Orrock the revolver – his name was McLellan – and he unhesitatingly identified bullets and cartridge cases as being the calibre of those he had sold to a young man in the last week of November 1882, one week before the murder. McLellan's description of the purchaser fitted Thomas Henry Orrock.

A few decades later, all this corroborative evidence would have been unnecessary. Examination of the bullets under a comparison microscope would have proved that the bullet found in the tree at Tottenham was identical with the bullet that killed PC Cole. But in the year 1884, no one had yet thought of studying the pattern of rifle marks on the side of a bullet; it would be another five years before Professor Alexandre Lacassagne would provide the evidence to convict a murderer by studying bullet grooves under a microscope. Nevertheless, when Tom Orrock came to trial in September 1884, it was the bullet evidence that carried most weight with the jury. The bullet found in the tree at Tottenham was "precisely similar to the one found in the brain of the dead constable", said the prosecution. "If the prisoner purchased the revolver, where was it? A man did not throw away a revolver that cost him 10 shillings without good cause." The jury was convinced. On Saturday 20 September 1884, Thomas Orrock was convicted of the murder of PC Cole and sentenced to be hanged. The jury added a special recommendation to Sergeant Cobb for his persistence in tracking down the killer. But the chronicler relates that, in after years, Inspector Glass liked to claim credit for capturing Orrock, and "has often remarked that the man who in reality put the police in possession of their information to this day is ignorant that he disclosed to them this knowledge" – from which it would appear that Glass continued to resent the success of his subordinate and to deny him any of the credit.

chapter seven

THE MYSTERY OF JACK THE RIPPER

*B*y the 1880s, the Age of Gaslight was drawing to a close. In 1881, Edison developed the first electric power plant in the world. In 1890, electric lights were switched on in the Chamber of Horrors at Madame Tussaud's waxworks in London – they had to be shaded in green to produce the same "creepy" effect as the flickering gaslamps.

But the most sensational British crime of the century occurred in the final years of the gaslamp. The nature of the crimes was so horrific that the soubriquet of the unknown murderer was soon famous around the world.

Jack the Ripper

In view of our complete ignorance of the identity of Jack the Ripper, it is strange that the case has continued to exercise such fascination for over half a century. Many people suppose that the Ripper crimes took place over many years and that his victims ran into dozens; whereas, in actual fact, the murders took place over a few months in 1888 and the victims were certainly not more than seven in number – quite possibly only four. The present writer has read an article in a spiritualist newspaper called *Two Worlds*, in which it is alleged that a medium, Mr Lees, helped to catch the Ripper; the article speaks of the murders as extending over several years and running into hundreds. Similarly, an article in the surrealist magazine of the 1920's, *Minotaur*, by Maurice Heine, speaks casually of "the eleventh victim", and includes a dubious photograph of the "eleventh victim".

The facts, briefly, are these: between 31 August 1888 and 8 November 1888 five murders took place within an area of half a mile in Whitechapel in the East End of London. All the women were mutilated with a knife and on several occasions some of the internal organs were taken away. After 8 November the murders ceased abruptly.

During the early part of 1888 there were two murders of women in Whitechapel that may possibly have been the work of the Ripper. The first was of an unfortunate woman named Emma Elizabeth Smith, aged forty-five, who was returning home in the early hours of the day following Easter Monday (3 April) when she was attacked. Twenty-four hours later she died in hospital of peritonitis, some sharp instrument like a spike having penetrated her abdomen. She claimed she was attacked by four men in Osborn Street at about four in the morning as she was returning home from a public house; they took her money (only a few coppers) and mistreated her. Her account of the four men seems circumstantial enough; she described one of them as being only nineteen.

The murder which is often regarded as the Ripper's first crime took place in Gunthorpe Street (then known as "George Yard") in the early hours of the day following Bank Holiday Monday, 7 August. A prostitute named Martha Turner (or Tabram) was picked up by a soldier on Bank Holiday night and seen in The Angel and Crown drinking with him. Several hours later (at about 5 a.m.) her body was found on the first landing of George Yard Buildings. She had been stabbed thirty-nine times; the murderer had used two weapons, one a bayonet or long-bladed knife, the other some kind of surgical instrument. He was also ambidextrous. The soldier who had been seen with her was traced, but had an alibi; all the soldiers in the Tower were paraded, but no arrest was made. It is impossible to state with any certainty whether this was the Ripper's first crime in Whitechapel, but most writers on the case are inclined

to believe that it is the work of the Ripper. The present writer
is inclined to doubt it.

At 2.30 a.m. on Friday 31 August, a woman friend saw a
prostitute named Mary Anne Nicholls (known as "Polly") at
the corner of Osborn Street; she admitted to having had "no
luck". Three-quarters of an hour later, her body was found
by a carter named Cross in Bucks Row (now called Durward
Street), lying in the entrance to the Old Stable Yard at the west
end of the street. In the mortuary of the Old Montague Street
Workhouse it was discovered that she had been disembowelled.
Death was due to severing of the windpipe. She was identified
by her husband, a printer's machinist, from whom she had been
separated for seven years. She was forty-two years of age, and
known as a habitual drunk. When her husband saw her body,
he was heard to say, "I forgive you for everything now I see
you like this." It was revealed that she had been staying at
a dosshouse in Thrawl Street, where a bed could be had for
fourpence a night. On the previous evening she had been
turned away from the dosshouse because she had no money.
She commented, "Don't worry, I'll soon get the money. Look
what a fine bonnet I've got."

A bruise on her face indicated that the murderer clamped
his hand over her mouth before cutting her throat. A woman
sleeping in a bedroom only a few yards from the murder heard
no sound.

The next murder took place on 8 September. Annie Chapman,
aged forty-seven was turned away from a lodging house in
Dorset Street, having no money to pay for a bed. It seems
probable that the murderer accosted Chapman outside the
yard where the murder took place – at 29 Hanbury Street.
She accompanied him down a passageway at the side of the
house some time after 5 a.m. The body was found shortly after
6 a.m. The head had been almost severed from the body, and
then tied in place with a handkerchief. The body was cut open,
as in the case of Mary Nicholls, and the kidney and the ovaries
had been removed. Two front teeth were missing (repeating a
curious feature of the Nicholls murder) and two brass rings
and some coppers were laid at her feet. In another corner
of the yard was the torn corner of a bloodstained envelope,
containing the crest of the Sussex regiment. Under a tap was a
leather apron. It seems possible that these last two items were

intended to mislead the police. A soldier had been suspected in the Tabram case, and Whitechapel gossip named a man called "Leather Apron" as the murderer. (He was actually a Polish Jew named Pizer, a shoemaker, who was arrested and then released.) Again the murderer had carried out the crime with extreme coolness and had made no sound. There were sixteen people living at 29 Hanbury Street and a scream would have quickly brought help to the victim.

On 28 September a letter was sent to the Central News Agency signed "Jack the Ripper" and threatening more murders. "I am down on whores and shant quit ripping them till I do get buckled." Whether or not it was by a practical joker, the name caught the public imagination when it first appeared in the newspapers (after 30 September).

The murders caused a universal panic. Meetings were held in the streets, criticizing the police and the Home Secretary. Bloodhounds were suggested, but they promptly lost themselves in Tooting. The newspapers of the time gave extremely full reports of the murders and inquests, and were tireless in offering theories.

A description of the murderer offered by someone who saw Annie Chapman talking to a man outside 29 Hanbury Street included a large moustache and a "foreign appearance".

On the morning of 30 September two murders were committed in Whitechapel. The first was of a Swedish woman called Elizabeth Stride. A hawker named Louis Deimschutz drove his horse and cart into the back yard of the International Workers Educational Club in Berner Street. (A council school now stands on the site.) He saw a woman's body on the ground and rushed into the club to give the alarm. The woman's throat had been cut and she had been killed very recently – so recently that it is possible that "Jack the Ripper" was interrupted and made his escape as Deimschutz entered the club. This was at 1 a.m.

At this time a forty-three-year-old prostitute named Catherine Eddowes was released from Bishopsgate police station, where she had been in charge for drunkenness. She was picked up by the Ripper and taken into a narrow alleyway that extends between Mitre Square and Duke Street, known as Church Passage (now St James Passage). Police Constable Watkins passed through the passage on his beat at one-thirty. A quarter of an hour later he again passed through the square, and found the body of Catherine Eddowes in the corner of the square near Church Passage. Her face had been badly mutilated – perhaps to delay identification – and the body cut open in the usual way; the left kidney and entrails had been removed and taken away. It was some time before she was identified, and in the meantime, one of the newspapers published a report that she was thought to be a certain "Mary Anne Kelly". This is a

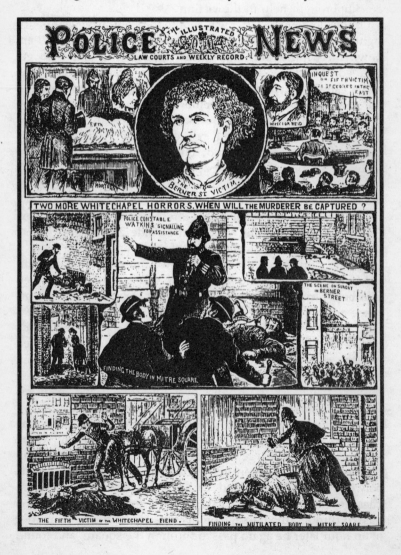

remarkable co-incidence, since the name of the final victim was Mary Jeanette Kelly.

A householder who lived in Berner Street (off the Commercial Road and the farthest afield of the Ripper's murders) testified that she saw a young man carrying a shiny black bag away from the scene of the crime. (Men carrying black bags were sometimes attacked in the street in Whitechapel at this time, and the Ripper murders made this type of bag go quite conclusively out of fashion.)

After the murder the Central News Agency received another letter signed "Jack the Ripper", regretting that he had been interrupted with his victims, and had not been able to send the ears to the police. (There had been an attempt to cut off the ear of Catherine Eddowes.) He also mentioned that "number one squealed a bit", which is borne out by a witness in Berner Street who heard the cry. The letter was posted only a few hours after the murders, and was written in red ink.

The murders had caused unprecedented excitement, and bands of vigilantes patrolled the streets of Whitechapel at night. But as weeks passed without further crimes, the panic died down. (One theory suggests that the Ripper was incarcerated in a mental home during these weeks.) On 9 November the last of the murders took place at a house in Millers Court, which ran off Dorset Street (now Duval Street), probably between Dorset Street and Whites Row to the south. Mary Jeanette Kelly was younger than the other victims, but of the same class. She was twenty-four. On the morning of 9 November at 10.45 a.m. a man knocked on the door of Mary Kelly to collect the rent. Getting no reply, he peered in at the broken window. What remained of Mary Kelly lay on the bed. The head had been almost severed from the body; the heart had been placed on the pillow. The entrails had been draped over a picture frame. The murderer had apparently worked by the light of a pile of rags, the ashes of which were burnt in the grate. Neighbours testified to hearing a cry of "Murder" at about 3.30 a.m. The inquest revealed that no parts of the body had been taken away this time.

The panic caused by the murder led to the resignation of Sir Charles Warren, the unpopular Chief of Police.

There were three other crimes that some writers on the case believe may have been committed by the Ripper. In June 1889,

The final words of Dr Neil Cream – poisoner of four London prostitutes in 1891 – were: "I am Jack the . . ."; then the trap dropped. *Could* Cream have been Jack the Ripper? Apparently not: he was in Joliet Penitentiary, in Chicago, serving a life sentence for poisoning a patient, at the time of the murders.

But a Canadian professor has noted that Joliet was a notoriously corrupt prison, where a rich prisoner could buy his freedom. And in 1897, the year before the Ripper murders, Cream's father died, and left him £5,000 . . .

So it is *just* possible that Cream's last words were true after all.

parts of a female body were found in the Thames. The head was not found, but a scar on the wrists enabled the police to identify the victim as Elizabeth Jackson, a prostitute who lived in a lodging house in Turks Row, Chelsea.

On 17 July the body of Alice McKenzie, known as "Clay Pipe Alice", was found in Castle Alley, Whitechapel; her throat was cut and there were gashes across her abdomen. In his introduction to *The Trial of George Chapman*, H. L. Adam quotes the McKenzie case as one of the Ripper murders.

Finally, on 13 February 1891, the body of Frances Coles, a prostitute of about twenty-five, was found under a railway arch at Swallow Gardens in Whitechapel; her throat had been cut and there were injuries to her abdomen. She was still alive when found, but died soon afterwards.

There have been many theories about the Ripper's identity. One of the earliest was put forward in 1929 in *The Mystery of Jack the Ripper* by Leonard Matters, a Member of Parliament. He claimed that the Ripper was a certain Dr Stanley, who had confessed to the crimes on his deathbed in Buenos Aires. According to Matters, Stanley's son had contracted syphilis from Mary Kelly – the last victim – and Stanley set out to track her down. Whenever he questioned a prostitute about her, he killed her so she could not warn Mary Kelly. And eventually he found Mary, and slaughtered her with vengeful ferocity . . .

Unfortunately, Dr Stanley is not to be found in the Medical Register for 1888, and was almost certainly a figment of Matters' imagination. Moreover, if Mary Kelly had been syphilitic, it would certainly have been recorded in the post mortem report.

What *was* noted in that report is that Mary Kelly was three months pregnant. And this led an artist named William Stewart to the conclusion that Jack the Ripper was a woman – a sadistic midwife, who had gone to Miller's Court to perform an abortion. To demonstrate that a woman would be capable of sadistic violence, he cites the case of Mrs Eleanor Pearcey, who killed the wife and baby of her lover Frank Hogg in October 1890, almost decapitating Phoebe Hogg. A bloodstained axe established her guilt and she was hanged on 23 December, 1890. But Mrs Pearcey's crime was committed out of jealousy. The notion of a female Jack the Ripper, killing out of pure sadism, is psychologically unrealistic.

A writer named William Le Queux had claimed in 1923, in *Things I Know*, that the Ripper was a mad Russian called Alexander Pedachenko, sent to London by the Tsar's secret police to embarrass the British police. He explained that he had unearthed this information in a manuscript on great Russian criminals written in French by the "mad monk" Rasputin, and discovered in the cellar of his house after his assassination in 1917. But Rasputin spoke no French, and his house did not have a cellar – he lived in a flat. In 1959, a journalist named Donald McCormick revived the Pedachenko theory, with "new evidence" from a manuscript called *Chronicles of Crime* by a Dr Thomas Dutton. But although Dutton certainly existed, his manuscript has vanished. And in 1988, the year of the Ripper centenary, McCormick declined to appear on television to defend his theory, which would seem to suggest that he has abandoned it.

One of the most interesting theories was first publicized by the television interviewer Dan Farson in 1959. Farson had tracked down the manuscript notes for *Days of My Years*, the autobiography of Sir Melville Macnaghten, the CID chief who joined Scotland Yard soon after the murders. Macnaghten mentioned that there were three major suspects, against two of whom "the case was weak". The third, who had committed suicide in the Thames soon after the last murder, was almost certainly – according to Macnaghten – Jack the Ripper. Macnaghten did not mention the actual names in his book.

Macnaghtens's original notes contained the three names; the two "weak suspects" were called Ostrog and Kosminksi, while the leading suspect was one "M. J. Druitt", "a doctor who lived with his family, and who drowned himself immediately after the murder of Mary Kelly."

Farson looked into the history of Montague John Druitt, and discovered that he was a barrister who committed suicide late in 1888. His career as a barrister had been a failure; he had taught in a private school in Blackheath, but had been dismissed for unknown reasons just before his suicide.

Both Farson and a journalist named Tom Cullen wrote books naming Druitt as the Ripper. But the objections against this are overwhelming. To begin with, it is obvious that Macnaghten is writing from mere hearsay. Druitt was not a doctor, he did not live with his family (he had rooms in the Temple), he did not commit suicide immediately after the Kelly murder, but a month later. We also know that he committed suicide because his mother had become insane, and he was afraid that the same thing was happening to him.

But perhaps the strongest objection to the Druitt theory is that Druitt was a member of the upper middle class. The study of "serial murder", which has received much attention in recent years, has revealed the interesting fact that all serial killers have been working class, and often suffered traumatic poverty and abuse in childhood. So far, at any rate, there has been no middle or upper class serial killer.

That observation also seems to dispose of an interesting theory held by a doctor named Thomas E.A. Stowell, who contacted the present writer in 1960. For various reasons, Stowell was convinced that Jack the Ripper was Queen Victoria's grandson, the Duke of Clarence, (known as Eddie), who would have become king of England if he had not died in the 'flu epidemic of 1892. Stowell had unearthed information that seemed to indicate that the Queen's physician, Sir William Gull, suspected Eddie of being the Ripper. He told me that Gull's private papers – which he had seen – revealed that Eddie had not died of 'flu, but of softening of the brain due to syphilis.

Stowell swore me to silence – in case it "upset her majesty" – but in 1970, finally published his theory in a magazine called *The Criminologist*. He called his suspect "S", but dropped enough hints to make it clear that he had Eddie in mind. The tremendous public furore that resulted – the story appeared in newspapers all around the world – killed him soon after the article appeared.

Another expert on the Victorian period, Michael Harrison, studied Stowell's article and decided that Stowell had misread Sir William Gull's papers, and that "S" was not the Duke of Clarence. It was probably Gull himself who referred to the suspect as "S"; but why call Clarence "S" when his name was Eddie? Harrison concluded that "S" was, in fact, Eddie's close friend (and tutor) James Kenneth Stephen, who died insane after a blow on the head from the vane of a windmill. Harrison unearthed some fascinating information about Stephen (the cousin of novelist Virginia Woolf, who also had mental problems and committed suicide), including some oddly sadistic poetry about women. But Jim Stephen sounds nothing like the descriptions of the Ripper given by woman who saw him. And if the observation that serial killers tend to be working class is correct, then his upper class origins make him a highly unlikely candidate.

Clarence was involved in a complicated theory put forward by journalist Stephen Knight in *Jack the Ripper: The Final Solution*, in 1976. According to Knight – who based his theory on the statements of a man called Joseph "Hobo" Sickert, son of the painter Walter Sickert – Clarence had secretly married an artist's model named Annie Crook. When the Palace found out, the model was kidnapped and confined in a mental home, and Sir William Gull was entrusted with the task of murdering Mary Kelly and a number of other prostitutes who knew the secret and were trying to blackmail the Palace. He did this in association with a coachman called John Netley, killing the women in the coach, and leaving deliberate clues associated with Freemasonry.

There is, in fact, some evidence that Clarence was the father of an illegitimate child, who in turn became the mother of "Hobo" Sickert. But Sickert himself admitted that the rest of his story – about Jack the Ripper – was a hoax. This should have been clear all along from the fact that Gull suffered a stroke in the year before the murders.

In the year of the Ripper centenary, a television production company, David Wickes Productions, announced that it had gained access to "secret Ripper files" and had established his identity beyond all possible doubt; this would be revealed in a fictional "documentary" in which Michael Caine would play Inspector Abblerline, the officer in charge of the case. The production company was later forced to acknowledge that their claims were "less than truthful", and to make a shamefaced climb-down. When the "documentary" finally appeared, it proved to be a well scripted but almost totally fictional account of the murders, in which Jack the Ripper proved to be Sir William Gull, in association with John Netley. All reference to the Annie Crook theory of "Hobo" Sickert were dropped; Gull's motive was reduced to insanity. As entertainment it was excellent; as a serious study of the murders, it must be dismissed as spurious and exploitatory.

Another Ripper expert, Robin Odell, advanced the theory that the killer was a Jewish slaughterman, a *shochetz*, who used ritualistic slaughter techniques on his victims; he defended this notion in *Jack the Ripper: Summing Up and Verdict*, (1988) co-authored with myself. The problem with Odell's interesting theory is that his evidence is purely circumstantial; all Whitechapel records that might have proved the existence of his hypothetical *shochetz* have been destroyed.

In *The Crimes, Detection and Death of Jack the Ripper*, Martin Fido, has argued that "Kosminski", another of Macnaghten's three suspects, was "Jack the Ripper, on the evidence of remarks made by Sir Robert Anderson, Assistant Commissioner of Police, who is recorded as saying that Jack the Ripper was a Polish Jew. Fido tracked down information about a man named Aaron Kozminski, who was committed to an asylum in 1891, and speculated that he might have been identical with a violent madman named David Cohen and a syphilitic named Nathan Kaminsky. Once again, the problem is simply lack of any concrete evidence to connect the suspects with the murders.

In *The Ripper Legacy*, Martin Howells and Keith Skinner return to Farson's theory that Druitt was Jack the Ripper, and add the speculation that he was murdered by former Cambridge friends to prevent the scandal from becoming known. Their research is excellent, but does not overcome the objections to the Druitt theory stated above.

Equally well researched is Melvin Harris's book *Jack the Ripper: The Bloody Truth*. He takes up a theory first advanced by the "magician" Aleister Crowley, and later elaborated by Richard Whittington Egan, to the effect that the Ripper was a doctor and adventurer named Roslyn D'Onston Stevenson, who committed the murders as part of a ritual to obtain "supreme magical power". Stevenson actually existed, but is on record as believing that the Ripper was a doctor named Morgan Davies. There is no real evidence to identify D'Onston (as he preferred to call himself) as the Ripper, and if the "working class" theory is correct, then it is virtually impossible, since he was from a wealthy middle class background. The same objection applies to a theory put forward by Jean Overton Fuller to the effect that the painter Walter Sickert was himself Jack the Ripper.

Other candidates for "Ripperhood" include John Netley himself (Tim Wright), Mary Kelly's common law husband Joseph Barnett (Bruce Paley) and Oscar Wilde's artist friend Frank Miles (Thomas Toughill). In all three cases, the evidence offered is once again purely circumstantial, without the kind of concrete facts that might support it. In the opinion of the present writer, the likeliest candidate is the father of a seventy-seven year old man who wrote to Dan Farson from Melbourne, Australia, and signed himself G.W.B. The letter reads:

> "When I was a nipper about 1889 I was playing in the streets about 9 p.m. when my mother called, 'Come in Georgie or JTR will get you'. That night a man patted me on the head and said, 'Don't worry Georgie. You would be the last person JTR would touch'." (This man was apparently the writer's own father.) "I could not remember the incident but it was brought to my mind many years later. My father was a terrible drunkard and night after night he would come home and kick my mother and us kids about something cruelly. About the year 1902 I was taught boxing and after feeling proficient to hold my own I threatened my father that if he laid a hand on my mother or brothers I would thrash him. He never did after that, but we lived in the same house and never spoke to each other. Later, I emigrated to Australia. I was booked to depart with three days' notice and my mother asked me to say goodbye to my father. It was then he told me his history and why he did these terrible murders, and advised me to change my name because he would confess before he died. Once settled in Melbourne I assumed another

name. However my father died in 1912 and I was watching the papers carefully expecting a sensational announcement". But this never came; his father died without confessing.

In Melbourne, "Georgie" changed his name, but after the death of his father, changed it back again.

"Now to explain the cause of it all. He was born 1850 and married 1876 and his greatest wish was his first-born to be a girl, which came to pass. She turned out to be an imbecile. This made my father take to drink more heavily, and in the following years all boys arrived. During the confession of those awful murders, he explained he did not know what he was doing but his ambition was to get drunk and an urge to kill every prostitute that accosted him."

Georgie's father seems to have been a collector of horse manure. On one occasion, after killing a woman, he was wearing two pairs of trousers. He removed the bloodstained outer pair and buried them in the manure. Later, when he and his mate stopped at the Elephant and Castle, where they usually ate sausage and mash, his father told his mate he was not hungry, and would bury himself in the manure to keep warm. While he was hidden there he heard a policeman asking questions about Jack the Ripper, and was "scared to death".

This letter certainly sounds authentic, and it is hard to imagine why a seventy-seven-year-old man in Melbourne should take the trouble to write a long anonymous letter if it was not true – it could hardly be a craving for attention. (Presumably, in spite of the anonymity, it should not be too difficult to discover G.W.B's name by studying sailing lists of ships to Melbourne in 1902.) Assuming, then, that "Georgie" believed every word he wrote, is it not conceivable that his father invented the story about being Jack the Ripper simply to get a kind of revenge on his son after years of ignoring one another? This is obviously a possibility. Yet in all other ways, Georgie's father sounds like the kind of suspect who *could* be Jack the Ripper – a highly dominant type, a heavy drinker, a bully where his family was concerned, and capable (as Charlotte MacLeod suggested) of holding down a job. Many serial killers and sadists have been heavy drinkers and have committed their acts of violence when drunk. If Georgie's father was not Jack the Ripper, then it is at least possible to state that he was the type of person who easily *could* have been. That is probably as far as we shall ever be able to go in solving the problem of the identity of the most notorious killer of all time.

Perhaps the most sensible comment on the identity of Jack the Ripper was made by London policeman Donald Rumbelow, author of *The Complete Jack the Ripper*. He remarked that if, on the Day of Judgement, the Archangel Gabriel says: "Stand forth, Jack the Ripper, and tell us your name", everybody in the audience will say: "*Who*?"